EXMOO|

Jonathan White

EXMOOR
BOOKS

© Jonathan White

First published 1994

EXMOOR BOOKS
Dulverton, Somerset

Trade sales enquiries:
Westcountry Books
Halsgrove House
Lower Moor Way
Tiverton. EX16 6SS

Tel: (0884) 243242
Fax: (0884) 243325

Exmoor Books is a Partnership between
The Exmoor Press and Exmoor National Park

British Library Cataloguing in Publication Data
A CIP Catalogue Record for this book is
available from the British Library

ISBN 0 86183 256 6

Front cover illustration: Pied Flycatcher.

Printed in Great Britain by
Longdunn Press,
Bristol

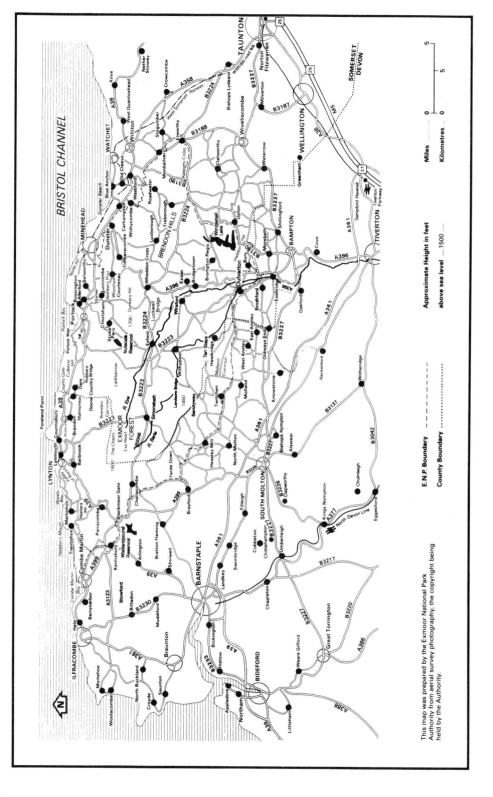

BRISTOL CHANNEL

This map was prepared by the Exmoor National Park
Authority from aerial survey photography, the copyright being
held by the Authority.

E.N.P. Boundary — — — — — — —

County Boundary ⋯⋯⋯⋯⋯⋯

Approximate Height in feet

above sea level ——— 1500 ———

Miles   0   5

Kilometres   0   5

CONTENTS

NOTE

This book is intended to provide a complete, up-to-date list of birds recorded on Exmoor, and their present status. This has involved compiling records and bringing together information from a number of sources — all of which are listed in the bibliography at the back of the book.

INTRODUCTION

Designated a National Park in 1954, Exmoor was the eighth area in Britain to be given such status. Its 692 square kilometres (267 square miles) contain a variety of landscapes and habitats which support an abundance of wildlife, many species of which are less common in other parts of the South West region than they are on Exmoor. About two thirds of the National Park lies in Somerset, the remainder being in Devon. The landscape can be roughly divided into five distinct types, each with its own diversity of wildlife.

These areas are:

> The Coast
> Farmland
> Woodland
> Rivers and Reservoirs
> Moorland

THE COAST

Exmoor has some 55 km (34 miles) of coastline, from Minehead in the east, to Combe Martin in the west, and about 15 km (9 miles) of this is designated a Site of Special Scientific Interest (S.S.S.I.). The whole of Exmoor's coast was designated a Heritage Coast in 1991.

The coast from Dunster Beach to Minehead consists mainly of sand and mud, vast areas of which are exposed at low tide providing a feeding area for many waders. Curlew, Ringed Plover, Oystercatcher, Turnstone and Dunlin are present most months (reaching a peak in autumn and winter), but a number of less common species can also be present at certain times of the year, including Knot, Whimbrel, Little Stint, Ruff and Curlew Sandpiper.

Away from the beach, the fields and hedges bordering the Minehead Golf Course, and the Dunster Hawn area, are good for migrants such as warblers, chats, redstarts and wagtails. In winter Snow Bunting is a regular visitor to this part of the coast, and divers and sea duck, (such as Common Scoter, Eider, Scaup, and - once - Velvet Scoter) have also been seen.

In spring and autumn, skuas and terns can be seen flying past out to sea (or resting on the mud, in the case of the terns). More uncommon species also occasionally turn up, with Firecrest, Yellow-Browed Warbler, Slavonian Grebe and Bittern having been seen at the Hawn. Iceland Gull, Glaucous Gull, and the more regular Mediterranean Gull can be found in the flocks of commoner gull species, while in 1989 Minehead Golf Course turned up an Isabelline Shrike to add to its older record of another national rarity — Cream-coloured Courser.

The coast west from Minehead to Combe Martin consists of steep rugged cliffs, (with the exception of the long shingle beach between Bossington and Porlock Weir), which are between 150m (500ft) and 305m (1000ft) high and include the highest cliffs in England, at Countisbury.

These cliffs, especially between Lynmouth and Heddon's Mouth, provide nest sites for Peregrines, Fulmars, Kittiwakes, Razorbills, and Guillimots, with a few pairs of Great Black-backed, and Herring Gull.

Behind the shingle bank of Porlock Beach lie the reed beds and open water of Porlock Marsh. This area is heavily disturbed by walking (and shooting, in winter), but an impressive list of rare birds have turned up there to complement the more regular species. These rarer birds include Blue-winged Teal; Terek, Pectoral and Baird's Sandpipers; Long-billed Dowitcher; Laughing Gull; White-winged Black Tern; Alpine Swift; and Rose-coloured Starling.

FARMLAND

There are 38,724 ha (95,685 acres) of farmland within Exmoor, mainly used for beef and sheep production, with some limited dairy and arable.

Although often considered unproductive in terms of wildlife, areas of farmland do support a wide range of species. Hedgerows, of which there are 5,500 km (3,400 miles) on Exmoor, often form the boundaries between fields providing breeding habitat for a number of smaller birds, including Blackcap and Garden Warbler. The remains of crops left in fields provide food for mixed flocks of finches, Brambling, larks and wagtails, which can get quite large especially in winter.

The short grass in grazed fields is also attractive to waders. Groups of Curlew, Lapwing, and Golden Plover, often totalling hundreds of birds, are regularly found on the lower lying coastal fields.

2

WOODLAND

Exmoor has a number of woodland areas, totalling 8,400 ha (20,800 acres) which is 12% of the area of the National Park. (This figure includes the main woodlands, and also the smaller woodlands, shelter belts and copses). Of this figure 3,000 ha (7,400 acres) is 'ancient woodland' which has existed since before 1600, and some of this is likely to have been continuously wooded since the last Ice Age.

Both oak woodland, (such as Horner Woods), and the coniferous plantations, (like the wooded area on Croydon Hill) are found on Exmoor. This coniferous woodland has mostly been planted since 1919, making up just under half of Exmoor's principal woodland.

The broad-leaved woodlands are more diverse in the number of species that they support, with all three woodpeckers, Nuthatch, Treekeeper, Tawny Owl, Buzzard, tits and finches all resident. Pied and Spotted Flycatchers, warblers, (notably Wood Warbler), and Redstarts breed in summer.

The coniferous woodland is not totally devoid of life however. Flocks of tits and Goldcrests can be seen flitting around at the treetops. Redpoll and Siskin are also present with Siskin breeding for the first time in conifers at Luccombe in 1979 — the first proven breeding record for Somerset also. Crossbills are also present in the conifer woods and the presence of juveniles indicate they too breed. In summer the 'churring' of Nightjars can be heard, this species breeding in woodland clearings and fringes.

RIVERS AND RESERVOIRS

There are some 480 km (300 miles) of rivers and major waters on Exmoor, including the three reservoirs of Wimbleball, Nutscale and Challacombe.

The eight principal rivers on Exmoor are the Avill, Barle, Bray, Exe, Haddeo, Lyn, Mole and Quarme. They are fed by numerous smaller streams which in turn are supplied by the rather wet climate that Exmoor has, with average rainfall on the Chains of 200 mm (80 inches).

Along the rivers species such as Dipper, Kingfisher, and Grey Wagtail breed. Recent surveys have found that Dipper and Grey Wagtail are maintaining their population and not experiencing a decline as in some other areas of the country.

Common Sandpiper, and less frequently Green Sandpiper, appear along the river edges of passage, and Sand Martins also breed, though not in the numbers that they previously did (in line with the general decline of this species across the country as a whole).

Of the reservoirs, Wimbleball is by far the biggest, with a capacity of 19,320 million litres (4,250 million gallons), and a surface area of 160 ha (370 acres), also being the best for birdlife.

In winter several species of duck are present in various numbers, largely depending on the weather conditions, with Mallard, Teal, Wigeon, Pochard, Tufted Duck, Goosander, and Goldeneye regular. Less regularly, Scaup, Gadwall, Shoveler, and Common Scoter turn up, while harsh weather brings in Ruddy Duck, Smew and Red Breasted Merganser. Rare ducks have also been seen such as Ring-necked Duck, and American Wigeon. The lake holds a large Canada Geese flock encompassing a number of 'exotic' geese, Bar-headed and Emperor for example. Egyptian Geese are also resident and have bred on occasions.

Few waders are found at Wimbleball in terms of numbers, but on passage Green, Common, and Wood Sandpipers, Greenshank, Spotted Redshank, and Little Ringed Plover have been seen, with Dunlin, Ringed Plover, and Redshank more regular. The habitiat around the lake provides suitable breeding habitat for a number of species, notably Wood Warbler, Pied Flycatcher, Whinchat, Raven and Willow Tit.

The other reservoirs are smaller, Nutscale having a capacity of 177 million litres (39 million gallons), and Challacombe 52 million litres (11.5 million gallons). They do not have such a wide range of species as Wimbleball, but Nutscale has had Scaup, Pochard, and Goosander. The surrounding area holds Buzzard, Raven, Redstart, Grey Wagtail, Dipper, Cuckoo, and various warblers and pipits, as well as commoner species.

MOORLAND

19,000 ha (46,900 acres) of moorland exist on Exmoor, a much reduced amount from the 30,400 ha (75,100 acres) that existed at the turn of the century. This landscape is often harsh and inhospitable especially in winter. As a result resident birds often move down to lower altitudes at that time of year.

Meadow Pipit and Skylark are resident, and Red Grouse retain a slender foothold on the slopes of Dunkery. (Black Grouse were also seen frequently 20 years ago, but they are now extinct, the last one being seen in 1981).

In the summer the moorland comes alive, with Stonechat, Tree Pipit, Whinchat, Wheatear, Ring Ouzel, Cuckoo, Curlew, and Lapwing being among the species that breed. Exmoor has a good representation of raptors, with Hobby and Merlin breeding on the moor as well as the Buzzards, Kestrels, and Sparrowhawks.

On passage Snow Bunting and Dotterel are occasionally seen, while winter brings flocks of thrushes to the combes in search of berries. Single Hen and Montagu's Harriers, Red Kite, and Great Grey Shrike are regularly seen on the moor. Arguably, though, the most exciting bird the moor has ever hosted is the Snowy Owl, for which there are a few old records.

LAYOUT OF THE BOOK

RED-THROATED DIVER (Gavia stellata) [W], [RP]
(SPECIES AND LATIN NAME)

J F M A M **J J A S** O **N D**

The [W], [RP] denotes the status as per the legend below. The letters in the box relate to the months of the year. An underlined letter denotes the months in which the species is usually recorded. An outlined letter denotes the months when species is rarely or occasionally seen. In this example the species is a winter visitor, rare passage migrant usually recorded in January - March and November and December, occasionally seen in April, May and October.

[V] = Vagrant   [RW] = Occasional/Rare Winter Visitor

[W] = Winter Visitor   [RP] = Occasional/Rare Passage Migrant

[P] = Passage Migrant   [RS] = Occasional/Rare Summer Visitor

[S] = Summer Visitor   [RB] = Rare Breeder/has bred in the
                                        past but no longer
[B] = Breeding Species   [RR] = Rare Resident

[R] = Resident

SYSTEMATIC LIST

The systematic list follows the sequence and scientific nomenclature of Dr K.H. Voous (1977, List of Recent Holarctic Bird Species).

RED-THROATED DIVER (Gavia stellata) [W], [RP]

J F M A M **J J A S** O **N D**

Singles and pairs seen off the coast west of Dunster most winters. Most records refer to wintering birds with some passage movement noted.

Away from the coast has been recorded at Wimbleball Reservoir, March 1983.

In the 10 years before 1988 an average of three records per year were seen off the coast. 141 divers were seen in 1988 however, in January and November/December with flocks of up to 240 divers wintering off Hartland Point, Devon, January 1988. R.T. Divers are probably more frequent off Exmoor's coast than records would suggest.

BLACK-THROATED DIVER (Gavia arctica) [W]

J F **M** A **M J J A S O N** D

Rare visitor to Exmoor, with the only records in the past 10 years being:

- two at Wimbleball, February 16-21st 1985
- one at Dunster Beach, December 15th 1985
- one at Porlock Weir, February 7th 1988
- one at Dunster Beach, February 3rd 1990
- two at Porlock Bay, April 28th 1990
- one at Minehead on January 26th 1991.

GREAT NORTHERN DIVER (Gavia immer) [RW]

J F M A M J J A S O N D

Very rare visitor to Exmoor. Six recent records:

- one at Dunster Beach, December 21st and 31st 1985
- one at Dunster Beach, January 11th 1986
- one at Porlock Bay, December 23rd 1987
- an unusual record of an April bird at Wimbleball, on April 20th 1987
- one at Porlock Bay, January 1st 1990, and one there on January 10th
- one at Porlock Weir on January 10th 1990.

Great Northern Diver

LITTLE GREBE (Tachybaptus ruficollis) [RB], [W]

J F M A M J J A **S O N D**

Has bred on Exmoor in the past, including at Dunster Hawn, but it is not a regular breeding species. Mainly a scarce winter visitor with up to ten at Wimbleball and smaller numbers, or singles at Porlock Marsh and Dunster Hawn.

———————

GREAT CRESTED GREBE (Podiceps cristatus)
[RB], [R], [W]

J F M A M J J A S O N D

Irregular on Exmoor except at Wimbleball, where up to six are present most months. A pair nested successfully there in 1985, the first breeding record. Singles are also recorded off the coast of Dunster, Hurlstone and Porlock.

———————

RED-NECKED GREBE (Podiceps grisegena) [RW]

J F **M A M J J A S O N** D

Very rare winter visitor. Only recorded from Porlock Marsh:

- one there, February 14th 1956.

———————

SLAVONIAN GREBE (Podiceps auritus) [RW]

| J | F | M | A | M | J | J | A | S | O | N | D |

Also a rare winter visitor, although more frequent than Red-necked Grebe:
- one at Minehead Clay Pits, January 9th 1960
- one at Dunster Hawn, October 7th 1972.

BLACK-NECKED GREBE (Podiceps nigricollis) [RW]

| J | F | M | A | M | J | J | A | S | O | N | D |

Similar in status to Slavonian Grebe, also being more frequent than Red-necked Grebe.

- one at Minehead Clay Pits, July 12th 1959
  (probably a stray passage bird)
- two at Porlock Marsh, February 22nd 1985.

FULMAR (Fulmarus glacialis) [B], [S]

| J | F | M | A | M | J | J | A | S | O | N | D |

Bred for the first time in 1958 at Martinhoe. Now some 300 pairs breed between Lynton and Heddon's Mouth, with 350 pairs in 1992. The first record of breeding for Somerset Exmoor was in 1981 at Glenthorne, where two pairs bred, and where breeding has occurred since. In 1986 and 1987 a pair prospected at Culver Cliff (Minehead), but breeding hasn't occurred there yet. Also seen off the coast out of the breeding season, and large numbers are often seen in gales, as on July 25th 1977 when 120 were present in Porlock Bay.

CORY'S SHEARWATER (Calonectris diomedea) [V]

J	F	M	A	M	J	J	A	S	O	N	D

Rare vagrant with two records of five birds seen off the coast:

- four off Lynmouth, August 26th 1986
- one down channel off Minehead, September 6th 1987.

GREAT SHEARWATER (Puffinus gravis) [V]

J	F	M	A	M	J	J	A	S	O	N	D

Very rare, with only one record of two off Lynmouth, August 26th 1986. No records from the Somerset Exmoor coast.

Great Shearwater

SOOTY SHEARWATER (Puffinus griseus) [V]

J F M A M J J A S O N D

Rare, offshore vagrant, with three records of nine birds:
- one Porlock Bay, September 23rd 1972
- seven off Minehead, August 9th 1979
- one down channel, Porlock Bay, August 2nd 1987.

14

MANX SHEARWATER (Puffinus puffinus)   [S], [P]

J	F	M	A	M	J	J	A	S	O	N	D

Regular off the coast, on passage to and from Welsh breeding grounds, and also on feeding flights.

Numbers of up to 200 recorded most years, with larger numbers in some years as in 1986 when 350 were seen between Minehead and Porlock on August 7th alone. June 15th 1986, 280 plus were seen feeding off Glenthorne, probably a regular feeding movement.

In 1989 there were five counts of over 100 in Porlock Bay between June 10th and July 2nd — the highest being June 24th when 425 passed east and 233 west in two hours. There are two records of 100 plus, both Porlock Bay, June 5th 1977 and July 1988 (when 1,225 moved up channel).

MEDITERRANEAN SHEARWATER
(Puffinus yelkouan) [V]

J	F	M	A	M	J	J	A	S	O	N	D

This species has only recently been split from Manx Shearwater by the Records Committee of the British Ornithologists Union (see the October 1991 issue of *Ibis*). There is one record of the rare Balearic Shearwater (Puffinus yelkouan mauretanicus), of two off Minehead, June 1st 1958.

STORM PETREL (Hydrobates pelagicus) [V]

J F M A M J J A S O N D

Usually an autumn storm vagrant, although has been seen in all months from May to September. There is an old record of one early bird in Porlock Bay, May 7th 1928. Five records of six birds in the last 10 years, three in Porlock Bay (September 3rd 1983, August 7th 1986 and May 31st 1988), and two from Minehead (one September 5th 1983 and two August 7th 1986). Many probably go unrecorded in Porlock Bay however.

LEACH'S PETREL (Oceanodroma leucorhoa) [V]

J F M A M J J A S O N D

Very rarely seen off the Exmoor coast with most being of autumn storm vagrants. There is one spring record, of one in Porlock Bay, May 7th 1928. Only two records since 1967, both in Porlock Bay.

GANNET (Sula basana) [S], [P]

J F M A M J J A S O N D

Seen offshore most years April-September. Rare October-March, usually storm blown adults. Bred on Lundy until 1903. Now, however, the nearest gannetry is in South West Wales, where breeding numbers have increased in recent years.

Much commoner in some years than others, presumably because of the distribution of fish stocks, especially mackerel. In 1966 birds were regularly seen fishing for mackerel in Porlock Bay. Most records are of fewer than ten birds, but much higher numbers recorded after gales e.g:
- 130 Porlock Bay, September 3rd 1967
- 70 Porlock Bay, August 7th 1986.

One found dead on Minehead Beach, November 15th 1987.

CORMORANT (Phalacrocorax carbo) [R], [B]

| J | F | M | A | M | J | J | A | S | O | N | D |

Cormorant

Recorded most months in coastal areas and at Wimbleball. Winter numbers at Wimbleball have been increasing in recent years, probably due to the Water Authority abstaining from shooting. Numbers there up to 18 in winter, with a few also at Dunster Beach and along the coast.

Has bred at Martinhoe, Foreland Point (one pair in 1989), Lynmouth-Heddon's Mouth (one pair in 1989) and North Cleeve, near Trentishoe (five pairs in 1989).
Shooting at Wimbleball by the Water Authority has led to birds being recovered that had been ringed on the Solway Firth, the Dyfed Coast and Ulster.

SHAG (Phalacrocorax aristotelis) [B], [R]

J F M A M J J A S O N D

Rarer than cormorant, especially inland. Seen fairly frequently in Porlock Bay, and less frequently off Minehead and Dunster. Three or four breeding pairs between Lynmouth and Heddon's Mouth 1989. Outside the breeding season numbers usually less than three, although a flock of immatures in Porlock Bay, September 5th 1980, contained 49 birds.

BITTERN (Botaurus stellaris) [RW]

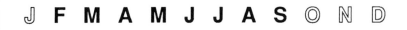

A rare winter visitor to Exmoor, most records being from Porlock Marsh and also Minehead Marshes/Dunster Hawn.

Has also been recorded near Dulverton, and in recent years, one was seen to fly down and land in the stream below Chetsford Bridge (an unusual site), where it was photographed, October 23rd 1989 (the most recent record, and only one in recent years).

AMERICAN BITTERN (Botaurus lentiginosus) [V]

J F M A M J J A S ◎ N D

The only record is of one shot on moorland near Parracombe, at the end of October 1875.

LITTLE EGRET (Egretta garzetta) [V]

J F M A Ⓜ Ⓙ Ⓙ A S O N D

Little Egret

19

Very rare visitor to Exmoor with only four records (of up to seven birds) most at Porlock Marsh:

- one, May 12th-14th 1979
- three, July 31st 1991
- a single or two together at Porlock Marsh on various dates in the spring of 1993
- one at Minehead on July 23rd 1993.

GREY HERON (Ardea cinerea) [R], [B]

J F M A M J J A S O N D

Away from the Heronries, singles seen along rivers and the coast. Numbers at Wimbleball reached up to 12 (December 13th 1987) but numbers at the lake have declined noticeably since. 13 on Dunster Beach September 5th 1989 was unusual with numbers of less than five more usual along the coast, although up to 40 have been seen at Porlock Marsh in August.

There are four main heronries in Exmoor: at Coppleham Cross, Winsford (founded pre-1965, maximum recorded number of nests = 28 (1971) and number of nests in 1987 = ten); Hayes Wood, Withypool (founded c. 1976, maximum recorded number of nests = eight (1984) and number of nests in 1987 = six); Badgworthy (founded pre-1984, maximum recorded number of nests = 12 (1984) and number of nests in 1987 = 11); and Holnicote (founded in 1989 when there were two nests).

In 1989 a pair also bred at Porlock. There are also a number of deserted Heronries which have had more than 10 nests in the past, including Dulverton, (perhaps as early as 1545, certainly 1790-1962) and Knowle Hill, Dunster, (1857-1912, with up to 30 nests).

Breeding has also occurred at Castle Hill, Dunster (1917-24 and 1952-

61); Court Copse, Exford (pre-1917 and 1920-28, which at 305 metres was perhaps the highest English Heronry).

WHITE STORK (Ciconia ciconia) [V]

```
J  F  M  A  M  J  J  A  S  O  N  D
```

A single record of one roosting on the church at Withiel Florey on June 3rd and 4th 1971 may refer to an escaped bird, and not to a genuine vagrant.

SPOONBILL (Platalea leucorodia) [V]

```
J  F  M  A  M  J  J  A  S  O  N  D
```

Two old records of this species, one each for Porlock Marsh and Minehead.

MUTE SWAN (Cygnus olor) [R], [B]

```
J  F  M  A  M  J  J  A  S  O  N  D
```

In 1420 Mute Swans were recorded as being 'taken' on Porlock Marsh. Up to 12 birds seen regularly at Dunster/Minehead, and Porlock Marsh, and at other places along the coast, rare elsewhere. Breeds regularly at Dunster Hawn and Minehead Marshes. Breeding has also taken place at Porlock Marsh.

Very rare at Wimbleball with one on December 5th 1988 being only the second record for the reservoir.

BEWICK'S SWAN (Cygnus columbianus) [RW]

Rare winter visitor (but more frequent than Whooper Swan):

- eight at Minehead Marshes, February 1976
- one at Porlock Marsh, November 1976
- one at Porlock Marsh, April 1980
- three at Minehead Golf Course, March 4th 1985
- one at Dunster Beach, February 7th 1993.

WHOOPER SWAN (Cygnus cygnus) [RW]

J F M A **M J J A S O** N D

An irregular and rare winter visitor — but more records in past few years than of Bewick's Swan, with:

- two at Dunster Beach, April 8th 1988
- one at Porlock Marsh, November 15th 1989
- two at Porlock Marsh, November 1st-4th 1990.

One at the mouth of the Lyn, April 1984, was injured and died later.

BEAN GOOSE (Anser fabalis) [V]

J F M A **M J J A S O** N D

Very rare visitor to Porlock Marsh/Minehead Marshes:

- one at Minehead Marshes, March 24th 1947
- singles at Porlock Marsh, mid November-
December 1949, February 11th 1956, December
4th-25th 1961, March 15th 1963
- more recently, one of unknown origin was
present at Porlock Marsh during March and
April 1993.

PINK-FOOTED GOOSE (Anser brachyrhynchus) [V]

J F M **A M J J A S** O N D

Very rare winter visitor with records from Dunster Beach, Porlock
Marsh and Wimbleball:

- six at Porlock Marsh, March 9th 1947
- two at Dunster Beach, October 23rd 1949
- one at Porlock Marsh, February 13th 1956
- one at Wimbleball, December 30th 1991.

23

WHITE-FRONTED GOOSE (Anser albifrons)   [W]
Eurasian race (Anser albifrons albifrons)

J F M **A M J J A S O N** D

Between 1941 and 1967 a flock of between 10 and 200 regularly visited Minehead Marshes, occasionally reaching very large numbers such as 1,000 seen on February 4th 1945. With the building of the Butlin's camp in the mid 1960s, the area of marsh was reduced, resulting in a decline in numbers. Now a scarce winter visitor although small groups do occasionally appear.

Up until the mid 1980s only one record from Wimbleball, but in 1986 five were present from January 1st-February 18th, and a single was there January 7th 1987 with two on January 31st.

Other recent records include:

- 32 at Minehead, January 29th 1985
- five at Dunster Beach, February 24th 1986 (probably the same five that were present at Wimbleball)
- two at Minehead/Dunster Beach February 16th 1987 and one at the same place February 25th 1987
- two at Porlock Marsh December 2nd 1989 and one December 4th-6th the same year
- one at Wimbleball on December 30th 1991.

Greenland Race (Anser albifrons flavirostris)

Vagrant. Not recently recorded, the only record being of one at Minehead Marshes, December 28th 1952.

GREYLAG GOOSE (Anser anser) [RW]

J F **M A M J J A S O N D**

A rare winter visitor with records from Porlock Marsh, January 16th 1977 and January 10th 1987; Dunster Marsh, February 28th 1987; and Minehead Marshes, January 7th 1991. There is always doubt as to whether the birds are genuine wild birds from Scandinavia or Eastern Europe, or whether they originate from the feral population on Chilton Moor. However, the timing of records (i.e. all in winter) suggests they could be genuine wild birds.

CANADA GOOSE (Branta canadensis) [R], [B]

J F M A M J J A S O N D

Present all year at Dunster Marsh/Wimbleball. Numbers up to 200 plus in autumn and winter, possibly as many as 300, with 283 at Dunster Beach, October 11th 1989. Breeds at Wimbleball and near Brompton Regis, with young also seen at Somerwest World, where 30 juveniles were present May/June 1990.

Small numbers seen elsewhere including Porlock Marsh and Nutscale Reservoir. Also seen in flight anywhere along the flight path of birds commuting from Wimbleball to Dunster Beach.

Cackling Goose (Branta canadensis minima)

Vagrant. One bird of this smaller race was present at Wimbleball throughout 1983, and another was at Dunster Beach, September 24th 1989.

BARNACLE GOOSE (Branta leucopsis) [RW]

```
J  F  M  A  M  J  J  A  S  O  N  D
```

Scarce winter visitor. Post 1960 it is not possible to be sure whether records are of genuine wild birds, or escapees from collections.

Pre 1960 there were three records, one from Porlock Marsh, February 28th 1917; and two from Minehead Marshes, (January 21st-February 6th 1940 and March 8th-9th 1947.

Four were present at Wimbleball in the winter of 1980/81. Since then up to five and a hybrid have been resident with the Canadian Geese (and presumably they are escaped birds).

Other recent records of one near Dunkery Hill Gate January 15th 1989 and one at Porlock Marsh January 24th 1987.

BRENT GOOSE (Branta bernicla) [W]

```
J  F  M  A  M  J  J  A  S  O  N  D
```

Scarce winter visitor. Recorded at Minehead/Dunster beaches, Porlock Marsh and Wimbleball. Usually singles, or small parties of up to four; but two recent records of flocks of 10 and 20 birds at Dunster Beach, November 1983 and January 23rd 1985 respectively.

Where specified most records have been of the Dark Bellied form, except:
- one at Minehead Marsh, February 1953
- four at Porlock Marsh (three of which were together January 28th 1988)

26

- four at Dunster Beach, September 20th-21st 1992.

These three records concern the Pale Bellied Greenland and Canadian form.

EGYPTIAN GOOSE (Alopochen aegyptiacus)   [R], [B]

J F M A M J J A S O N D

Local and scarce. One pair nested at Wimbleball in an old Buzzard's nest in 1982 and raised four young (the first Exmoor breeding record). May have bred in 1983 and certainly did in 1986 (in an old crow's nest). Up to eight seen at Wimbleball, but usually less than this number, with singles or pairs commuting between Wimbleball and Dunster Marshes with the Canadian Geese.

SHELDUCK (Tadorna tadorna)   [R], [B]

J F M A M J J A S O N D

Before 1900 was a common breeding species along the coast in rabbit burrows, hollow trees and cliff crevices. The largest colony was on Minehead Warren (now the Golf Course). Since 1900 breeding records from the Dunster area (until 1945), Minehead to Bossington, and Porlock Marsh to Glenthorne. In 1989 a pair were at Nutscale, April 27th, and two were disturbed from the cliff at Culbone, May 10th. An adult with four young crossed the road at Alcombe heading for the sea, June 14th 1989.

Recorded at Wimbleball (where usually a winter visitor).

Numbers in winter build up along the coast with up to 60 at Dunster Beach.

Shelduck

MANDARIN DUCK (Aix galericulata) [V]

J F M A M J J A S O N D

The origin of Mandarins on Exmoor is always uncertain, so the one recorded male at Butlin's Lake, November 9th 1983, may have escaped from a local collection, or may have been a wanderer from the breeding population of South East England.

WIGEON (Anas penelope) [W]

J F M A M J J A S O **N D**

The commonest wintering duck along the coast, especially at Porlock and Minehead/Dunster, with good numbers wintering at Wimbleball also.

Numbers up to 700 at Dunster Beach (although as many as 1000 have been seen), and 150 at Porlock Marsh. Winter numbers at Wimbleball usually up to 300, with 600 there during January/February 1987 unusual.

AMERICAN WIGEON (Anas americana) [V]

J F M **A M J J A S O N** D

One male at Wimbleball, January 30th-March 20th 1987, and presumably the same one there December 28th 1987-March 24th 1988. A female was also claimed at Wimbleball in early 1988.

American Wigeon

GADWALL (Anas strepera) [RP], [W]

J F M **A M J J A** S O **N D**

A rare visitor to Exmoor, mainly in winter. Small numbers, usually up to five, winter at Wimbleball, with single birds or pairs at Dunster Beach, sometimes more as in the four present there, January 25th 1987.

TEAL (Anas crecca) [W]

J F M A M J J A **S O N D**

Has bred in the past, at Dunster (1945), Porlock (1920), and Weir Water (1923). Regular winter visitor now, to coastal marshes and inland waters. Numbers at Wimbleball vary, but up to 100 regular (or 150 occasionally).

Larger numbers present at Porlock and Dunster, with 100-300 regular at both places. More unusual were over 600 at Porlock Marsh, December 1981.

Green-winged Teal (Anas crecca carolinensis)

Vagrant. One record of this North American race, at Porlock Marsh on October 4th 1951.

MALLARD (Anas platyrhynchos) [R], [B]

J	F	M	A	M	J	J	A	S	O	N	D

The most numerous of Exmoor's resident wildfowl. Breeds at a number of places including moorland freshwater areas. Resident numbers complemented in winter by over-wintering birds. Winter numbers at Wimbleball regularly up to 200, with smaller numbers along the coast, an exception being 111 at Dunster Beach, September 11th 1989.

PINTAIL (Anas acuta) [RW]

J	F	M	A	M	J	J	A	S	O	N	D

Scarce, but fairly regular winter visitor, usually to Dunster Beach and Porlock, but occasionally Wimbleball. Numbers of up to ten have been seen, although this is unusual, and in recent years only singles and pairs regular with larger numbers usually related to harder weather.

GARGANEY (Anas querquedula) [RP]

J F M A M J J A S O N D

An unusual spring passage migrant with past records from Minehead and Dunster Marshes, but none in recent years. Small numbers have nested in North Somerset and South Devon, but no breeding records from Exmoor.

BLUE-WINGED TEAL (Anas discors) [V]

J F M A M J J A S O N D

One record of this North American vagrant, a male at Porlock Marsh, April 17th 1981.

Blue-winged Teal

SHOVELER (Anas clypeata) [W]

J F M A M J J A S O **N D**

Fairly frequent winter visitor along the coast, with up to 20 recorded, although the largest number in recent years is 11 at Dunster Beach, January 28th 1988. Winter numbers at Wimbleball rarely exceed 10. Has attempted to breed but without success.

POCHARD (Aythya ferina) [W]

J F M A M J J A **S O N D**

Regular winter visitor to Wimbleball, with up to 40 regular October-March, although higher numbers occur occasionally such as 98 in January 1989 and 88 on November 18th 1990. Singles occasionally remain into April but there has been no record of breeding.

Has been recorded in small parties (or less) at Porlock Marsh, Minehead and Dunster, although much less common on the coast than at Wimbleball, with coastal records usually associated with harsh weather.

RING-NECKED DUCK (Aythya collaris) [V]

J F M **A M J J A S** O N D

Three records of this North American duck, presumably of the same bird:

- one male at Wimbleball, November 19th 1988-March 27th 1989
- one male at the same place, November 11th-December 10th 1989
- one male again at Wimbleball intermittently between December 15th-31st 1989
- probably the same male again present at Wimbleball from December 15th 1990-January 20th 1991.

TUFTED DUCK (Aythya fuligula) [W], [R], [B]

J	F	M	A	M	J	J	A	S	O	N	D

Resident numbers are swelled by wintering birds to inland waters, with numbers at Wimbleball up to 100. Usually present in smaller numbers at Wimbleball all year, though sometimes absent in July and August. Rare on the coast with seven present at Dunster Hawn in the winter of 1970/71 being unusual. Occasionally recorded from Nutscale.

The first breeding record for this species was in 1989 when a pair and six young were present at Wimbleball.

SCAUP (Aythya marila) [RW]

J	F	M	A	M	J	J	A	S	O	N	D

Tufted Duck

Rare winter visitor to coastal areas, and Wimbleball (where singles are almost annual). Most records are of singles or of pairs, with one at Nutscale, January 19th 1991, unusual for there. Hybridization within the Aythya genus frequently occurs, and records of hybrids exist from Wimbleball, most recently of one on February 12th 1989.

EIDER (Somateria mollissima) [RW]

J F M A M J **J** A S O N D

Until recent years a very rare vagrant with only a few definite winter records (the first being a male in Porlock Bay February 9th-June 5th 1964). In recent years has been seen more regularly, (in line with a national increase in their numbers and the presence of over-wintering flocks off South Wales).

Since 1985 there have been six records of at least five individuals:

- one Minehead, January 22nd 1986
- one male Porlock Bay, August 7th - April 18th 1987 (joined by a female in 1987)
- a pair Porlock Bay, August 13th - September 28th 1987 (possibly the same pair)
- one immature male Dunster Beach, November 28th 1988
- one Porlock Bay, March 26th 1989
- one female off Minehead, December 23rd 1991.

LONG-TAILED DUCK (Clangula hyemalis) [V]

J F **M A M J J A S O** N D

Very rare visitor to coastal areas. No records for recent years. Usually singles although two have been recorded at Porlock Marsh.

COMMON SCOTER (Melanitta nigra) [P], [RW]

J F M A M J J **A S O N D**

Uncommon, but usually recorded off the coast annually, with records from all months, but rarer in the summer. Has also been recorded from Wimbleball.

Up to 1965 there were 22 records between Dunster and Porlock with three records of parties of 12 birds.

Usually seen in only small numbers at Wimbleball with 18 on November 14th 1983 exceptional.

On the coast numbers usually less than ten although occasionally more, such as 30 plus at Dunster Beach on August 7th 1987.

Has also been recorded inland (after gales) e.g. at Dulverton.

VELVET SCOTER (Melanitta fusca) [V]

J F M A M J J A S O N D

Vagrant. One record of a male off Dunster Beach, December 21st 1985.

GOLDENEYE (Bucephala clangula) [W], [P]

J **F** **M** A M J J A S ◎ **N** **D**

Regular winter visitor and rare passage migrant, at Wimbleball November-March with numbers usually less than ten. Rarer visitor to the coast with records of singles from Dunster Hawn and Porlock Marsh with singles also recorded at Nutscale Reservoir and the River Avill.

Goldeneye

SMEW (Mergus albellus) [RW]

J F **M A M J J A S O N** D

Very rare winter visitor to the coast and Wimbleball. Has been recorded in the past at Porlock Bay, Minehead Clay Pits and Dunster. Most recent record is of a female at Wimbleball, January 31st to February 4th 1987.

Smew

RED-BREASTED MERGANSER (Mergus serrator) [RW]

J F M A M **J J A S** O N D

Rare winter visitor to Exmoor with records from Porlock Bay, Dunster Hawn, Dunster Beach, Wimbleball and Glenthorne. In recent years six records:

- one at Dunster Beach, January 24th 1987
- four at Wimbleball, February 24th 1987
- one male at Porlock Weir, April 21st 1988
- one male at Glenthorne, May 4th 1988
- one 'redhead' at Dunster Beach, November 25th 1990
- two males in Porlock Bay on November 30th 1991.

Red-breasted Merganser

39

GOOSANDER (Mergus merganser) [W]

J F M A M J **J A S** O **N D**

Regular winter visitor with records from a number of places including Wimbleball, Nutscale, Dunster Beach, the River Barle and Malmsmead, with numbers at Wimbleball up to 40, but usually singles elsewhere, with five at Dunster Beach, January 21st 1979 exceptional (although up to four have been seen at Nutscale).

Has been recorded in spring and summer with two at Porlock Beach May 24th 1987, a female on the River Barle, May 18th 1988 and a female at Wimbleball, June 15th 1988.

There have been several recent records of Goosanders breeding in Devon, and some of Exmoor's fast flowing rivers would seem to be just as suitable for breeding habitats, but as yet there have been no Exmoor breeding records.

RUDDY DUCK (Oxyura jamaicensis) [RW]

J F **M A M J J A S O N D**

Rare, with the only records coming from Wimbleball. Up to six were present here January/February 1987, but apart from that records usually concern single birds.

HONEY BUZZARD (Pernis apivorus) [V]

J	F	M	A	M	J	J	A	S	O	N	D

Probably a regular, if scarce, summer visitor to the older wooded areas in the early part of the last century. One recent record of a single bird at Robber's Bridge, May 25th 1990.

RED KITE (Milvus milvus) [RP], [RW]

J	F	**M**	**A**	**M**	J	J	A	S	O	N	D

Scarce migrant with singles recorded most years in spring as birds on passage pass through to their Welsh breeding grounds. However, there are some winter records (Selworthy Beacon, December 6th-18th 1970; East Anstey January 13th 1971; Horner Hill, December 4th 1983 and Lype Hill, January 21st 1988). One in the Timberscombe area from October 1989 until at least February 1990 was wing tagged, and was a released bird, part of a joint NCC and RSPB project to reintroduce Red Kites into England and Scotland.

There is one record of a pair present on Exmoor, in August/September 1949. The most recent record is one over Badgworthy Water, September 23rd 1992.

WHITE-TAILED EAGLE (Haliaeetus albicilla) [V]

J	F	M	A	M	J	J	A	S	O	N	D

There have been no recent records of White-tailed Eagle on Exmoor - the only ones, (of which there are four) are from the period between 1811 and 1912.

MARSH HARRIER (Circus aeruginosus) [RP]

J	F	M	A	M	J	J	A	S	O	N	D

Rare visitor, usually on passage, to coastal areas such as Porlock Marsh, (although there are inland records). Most records concern juveniles and females. There is one record of a female spending the winter on Minehead Marshes, in 1973/74, last being seen April 17th 1974.

HEN HARRIER (Circus cyaneus) [RB], [W]

J	F	M	A	M	J	J	A	S	O	N	D

Bred on Exmoor fairly regularly until about 1900/1910 and possibly since. A regular visitor with a handful of records most years, mainly on the moor, but also from Porlock Marsh and North Hill. A large proportion of records concern males, some occasionally in May and June and also August.

MONTAGU'S HARRIER (Circus pygargus) [RP], [RB]

J	F	M	A	M	J	J	A	S	O	N	D

There are four breeding records for Exmoor (all before 1920)

- Dulverton, c. 1850
- Simonsbath, 1868
- 'Exmoor', 1890
- Minehead Marshes, 1920.

A pair were also present on Exmoor all summer in 1945. Since then an irregular visitor with records in recent years from Exford Common (male, March 24th 1986) and Porlock Marsh (immature, August 20th 1988). Most records concern single birds although in the past, spring passage groups of five and four were seen at Porlock Marsh in 1930 and 1931 respectively.

GOSHAWK (Accipiter gentilis) [V]

J	F	M	A	M	J	J	A	S	O	N	D

One at Pinkworthy Pond, September 15th 1960, was the first record of this species for Somerset. Other records come from Horner (June 17th 1962), and near Simonsbath (August 15th 1971). Is a very rare visitor to Exmoor with only a few records in recent years from Devon-Exmoor, Timberscombe and the Brendons. The most recent being a pair displaying on the Brendons on March 11th and April 7th 1990; and March 10th 1990 near Winsford.

SPARROWHAWK (Accipiter nisus) [R], [B]

J F M A M J J A S O N D

A relatively common raptor which breeds on Exmoor. Numbers have recovered after their decline in the 1950s. In winter tends to become widely distributed especially along the coast. Frequently predates in gardens, where Blackbirds, Pigeons, Tits, Robins and Collared Doves are the most common prey.

One was seen taking a Spotted Flycatcher's nest at Luxborough in 1988, which contained young, and as it flew off with the nest one fledgeling fell out, but the rest remained in the nest.

BUZZARD (Buteo buteo) [R], [B]

J F M A M J J A S O N D

Probably Exmoor's commonest bird of prey. Breeds from the wooded farmland to the tall trees in the higher combes. Numbers of up to ten regularly seen soaring together especially in spring. Estimates of breeding numbers suggest probably at least 50 pairs, although the actual number may be higher.

ROUGH-LEGGED BUZZARD (Buteo lagopus) [V]

J F M A **M J J A S O** N D

Only about ten Exmoor records up to 1976 with one seen regularly on the Brendons during the winter of 1973/74. Few records since, the most recent being in 1987 when one was seen over Porlock on January 6th, and possibly the same bird at Lynmouth in the afternoon of the 6th, where a 'funny looking Buzzard that hovered' was reported.

Another believed to be of this species was seen over Weir Water on April 5th 1987.

GOLDEN EAGLE (Aquila chrysaetos)

Although not accepted as having ever been recorded in Exmoor, and omitted from the *Birds of Somerset* (1988), E.W. Hendy mentions, in his book *Birds of Somerset and Other Folk* (1943), a sportsman who was concealed on Porlock Marsh waiting for duck when he saw a large bird fly over his head and land on the bank less than 20 yards from him where it remained for five minutes preening itself, and stretching its wings. The observer was sure about its identity being familiar with Golden Eagles in Scotland.

Interestingly also, in a letter to the *Exmoor Naturalist* (1991) Mr M.F. Twist states that a pair of Golden Eagles were seen above Grixy Combe on 7th, 9th, 12th and 13th of January 1905. They were apparently seen by three observers who were 'very keen naturalists'.

Mr Twist also says that four Golden Eagles were seen in the same place on April 25th 1905, again by three observers.

OSPREY (Pandion haliaetus) [RP]

| J | F | M | A | M | J | J | A | S | O | N | D |

A rare passage migrant to Exmoor, with only four records since 1979:
- one at Chalkwater, April 28th 1979

- one at Roadwater Fisheries, October 16th - 22nd 1980
- one at Roadwater Fisheries, October 1981
- one over the River Barle at Landacre Bridge, May 9th 1989.

KESTREL (Falco tinnunculus) [R], [B]

J F M A M J J A S O N D

Common throughout the whole of Exmoor, being a widespread breeder. A party of seven hunting at once over White Water on September 17th 1989 was unusual.

Kestrel

MERLIN (Falco columbarius) [R], [B]

J F M A M J J A S O N D

Scarce, with only a few pairs breeding annually on the Moor. Disturbance by the public, egg collectors and also birdwatchers hamper their success. In winter they tend to disperse from the high ground and hence out of the breeding season records are widespread with many from the coastal area.

HOBBY (Falco subbuteo) [S], [B]

J F M A M J J A S ◎ N D

A scarce summer visitor to Exmoor with many of the records coming from moorland areas. Has bred at Porlock Parks before 1912, and has bred since. Two at Minehead Beach on October 17th 1987 was an unusually late record.

GYRFALCON (Falco rusticolus) [V]

J F M A M J J A S O N D

One record, of an individual of the Greenland Race on Foreland Point, March 17th 1972

PEREGRINE (Falco peregrinus) [R], [B]

```
J F M A M J J A S O N D
```

Uncommon, but regularly recorded from coastal and inland sites, including Wimbleball. Bred along the coast from Minehead to Glenthorne in the 1960s, when numbers were reduced by pesticide. Numbers have now recovered with pairs breeding annually along the Exmoor coast.

In winter numerous coastal sightings include up to five between Hurlstone Point and Minehead on a number of occasions.

One was seen chasing a Dunlin at Dunster Beach, August 8th 1991, causing the Dunlin to 'ditch' into the sea where it remained while the Peregrine circled overhead. Once the Peregrine flew off the Dunlin allowed itself to be washed ashore where it started feeding apparently unharmed.

RED GROUSE (Lagopus lagopus) [R], [B]

```
J F M A M J J A S O N D
```

This species has fluctuated in numbers on Exmoor. It was introduced in the 1800s but not really established until the early 1900s. Numbers then fell due to war-time disturbance, before increasing again at the end of the War in 1945. In 1976 about 40 pairs bred in an area from Robin How to Black Barrow above Weir Water.

Drastic reduction has occurred and now only a handful remain, with extinction looking inevitable. Two were seen near Pinkworthy Pond on January 31st 1982, but apart from that all records come from the slopes of Dunkery. Disturbance is probably a major reason for their decline although it has been found that Red Grouse is a host to sheep ticks which transmit Louping Ill disease, which is often fatal to sheep. This tick is abundant where the Red Grouse live on Exmoor and might also be a reason for the decline of this species.

BLACK GROUSE (Tetrao tetrix) [RB], [Ex]

| J | F | M | A | M | J | J | A | S | O | N | D |

Fairly common up to 1918 when a serious decline began. Became increasingly confined to north-east Exmoor. Attempts to stop the decline in numbers by introducing hand-reared Scottish birds were unsuccessful and numbers continued to fall. The last Lek on the Moor was in 1972, the last breeding record was 1975 and the last sighting was of a female at Lucott Moor at dusk on July 29th 1981.

Black Grouse

RED-LEGGED PARTRIDGE (Alectoris rufa) [B], [R]

J F M A M J J A S O N D

Locally common, especially where reared as a game bird. Small coveys exist around Bossington and Roadwater with other sightings from Countisbury, Hawkcombe, Selworthy, Winsford, Luxborough, the Brendons, Brompton Regis and even one making its way along Periton Road towards Porlock on April 14th 1990.

GREY PARTRIDGE (Perdix perdix) [R], [B]

J F M A M J J A S O N D

Uncommon, and almost entirely confined to agricultural land with recent records from the Brendon Hills, Timberscombe, Withycombe, Luxborough and Kinsford Gate, and six in grass at Allerford, December 18th 1991. Some of these records probably refer to introduced birds.

A legal document shows evidence of Grey Partridges (and Pheasants) at Carhampton and Rodhuish as early as 1355.

QUAIL (Coturnix conturnix) [S], [B]

J F M A M J J A S O N D

Rare summer visitor. Once bred widely, on the Brendon Hills and in Porlock Vale in the nineteenth century; near Culbone in 1966, the Brendon Hills in 1976 and probably at Luccombe in 1980. Most birds are heard between June and August with an unusual April record of a bird calling at 1.30am at Holnicote, April 7th 1980.

1989 was an exceptional year for this species with at least 20 calling males over a wide area, between June 7th and August 17th.

PHEASANT (Phasianus colchicus) [R], [B]

| **J** | **F** | **M** | **A** | **M** | **J** | **J** | **A** | **S** | **O** | **N** | **D** |

Common except on the high moor, but most are reared as game birds now, in many parts of Exmoor. Tend to be absent from the Exmoor valleys, being most frequent in Porlock Vale, up to Webber's Post and along the south edge of the National Park.

WATER RAIL (Rallus aquaticus) [W], [RR]

| **J** | **F** | **M** | A | M | J | J | A | **S** | **O** | **N** | **D** |

Regular but scarce winter visitor to coastal marshes and the Brendon Hills. Have been summer records from Porlock Marsh since 1970, but no confirmed breeding records although it may have bred.

Most records come from Porlock Marsh and Dunster Hawn, although it has also been recorded at Roadwater, Allerford, Dunster, Bossington, Alcombe Marshes and Woodcombe Allers. Up to five recorded most years.

SPOTTED CRAKE (Porzana porzana) [V]

J F M A M J J A S O N D

Only three records of this species, all from Porlock Marsh:

- one, December 9th 1958
- one, September 30th - October 4th 1959
- one, August 7th 1971.

BAILLON'S CRAKE (Porzana pusilla) [V]

J F M A M J J A S O N D

A single record of one at Minehead on the 12th or 13th of November 1912.

CORNCRAKE (Crex crex) [RB], [RS]

J F M A M J J A S O N D

Fairly regular (although declining) up to 1954 in Porlock Vale, between Carhampton and Minehead, and around Brompton Regis. The last breeding record was in 1954.

Since then very rare with occasional birds heard calling in May and June with one picked up dead at Porlock, October 13th 1982.

Corncrake

MOORHEN (Gallinula chloropus) [R], [B]

J F M A M J J A S O N D

Locally common with breeding occurring around Minehead (at Butlin's) and Dunster, and occasionally at Wimbleball. Other scattered breeding records, mostly from low lying land, with Moorhens being rare or absent from moorland above 150m (500 feet).

COOT (Fulica atra) [W], [R], [B]

J F M A M J J A S O N D

Common on most areas of open water. Breeds at Wimbleball, Dunster Hawn and Butlin's (Minehead). Numbers in winter are boosted by immigrants, with Wimbleball regularly holding up to 250 (with 308 in January 1987).

Can also be common on the marshes in winter if flooding occurs.

OYSTERCATCHER (Haematopus ostralegus) [B], [R], [W]

J F M A M J J A S O N D

Common on the coast being present most months, with maximum numbers in winter when up to 150 regular along the coast, although 280 have been recorded.

Has nested at Woody Bay; and two adults with one young were present at Dunster Beach, May 28th 1990.

BLACK-WINGED STILT (Himantropus himantropus) [V]

J F M A M J J A S O N D

One record of a single bird at Porlock Marsh, July 23rd to August 4th 1960.

Oystercatcher

AVOCET (Recurvirostra avosetta) [V]

J F M A M J J A S O N D

Three Exmoor records concerning ten birds:

- single at Porlock Marsh, April 26th - 30th 1963
- single at Porlock Marsh, October 29th 1973
- eight drifting with the tide in Porlock Bay, December 3rd 1987.

STONE CURLEW (Burhinus oedicnemus) [V]

J F M A M J J A S O N D

55

Very rare with no records for many years. Single birds at Minehead, April 4th 1912 and Great Hangman near Combe Martin, August 26th 1944, being the most recent records.

CREAM-COLOURED COURSER (Cursorius cursor) [V]

| J | F | M | A | M | J | J | A | S | O | N | D |

A single record of one on Minehead Golf Course, September 24th - 26th 1941. This was also the first Somerset record.

Cream-coloured Courser

LITTLE-RINGED PLOVER (Charadrius dubius) [RP]

| J | F | M | A | M | J | J | A | S | O | N | D |

Rare passage visitor with records from Porlock Marsh (four April 9th 1968, one April 14th 1968, one April 18th 1979, one May 27th 1978, one May 7th 1985 and one August 12th 1990), Minehead (one August 22nd 1971), and Wimbleball (one April 25th 1982, one June 28th - September 11th 1982 and one March 31st 1990.)

RINGED PLOVER (Charadrius hiaticula) [R], [B], [P]

| J | F | M | A | M | J | J | A | S | O | N | D |

Common along the coast with maximum numbers in autumn/winter. Has bred at Porlock/Bossington Beach (probably last in 1981) and Dunster Beach. Up to 200 along the coast in autumn with smaller numbers present during the winter. Numbers at Wimbleball usually less than ten and mainly on autumn passage.

KENTISH PLOVER (Charadrius alexandrinus) [V]

| J | F | M | A | M | J | J | A | S | O | N | D |

Two records of this species:
- one at Porlock Marsh, April 19th 1956
- one at Minehead, November 10th - 12th 1968.

DOTTEREL (Charadrius morinellus) [RP]

| J | F | M | A | M | J | J | A | S | O | N | D |

Rare, but probably regular passage migrant. Most often seen in the Dunkery area with up to three seen fairly regularly. Has been recorded from other sites (including Minehead Golf Course, August 1969), with some larger groups such as the 22 on Chains Barrow, April 25th 1984; eight near Brendon Two Gates, April 1981, and seven at Robin How, May 1973.

GOLDEN PLOVER (Pluvialis apricaria) [W], [P]

| **J** | **F** | **M** | **A** | M | **J** | **J** | **A** | **S** | **O** | **N** | **D** |

Probably bred on Exmoor in 1910 (although not proved) but not since. Numbers in recent years much declined from the thousands that occurred at one time (for example 6,000 at Minehead, January 21st 1967). In spring up to 700 have been recorded with up to 300 regular on the moor. Since 1980 flocks have rarely exceeded 100-150 although numbers may be picking up with 420 at Minehead on October 13th 1989 and 500 at the same place, November 16th 1991.

Single birds occasionally seen on the high moor in early summer — probably late passage migrants as there have been no reports of breeding.

GREY PLOVER (Pluvialis squatarola) [W], [P]

J F M A M J J A S O N D

Uncommon, but regular with a maximum of 22 at Dunster/Minehead in January and infrequent at Porlock. In recent years up to seven at Dunster Beach and up to three at Porlock although usually singly or in pairs, with 21 at Dunster Beach, January 1986 being unusual. Has also been recorded on passage at Simonsbath.

LAPWING (Vanellus vanellus) [R], [B]

J F M A M J J A S O N D

Large winter flocks of up to 150 on many lowland fields and coastal marshes regular with well over 200 on Minehead Marsh, January 9th 1991. Breeds regularly at Porlock Marsh and Minehead, and also on the Brendons and the heathland, usually in colonies of three/four pairs in a few places on the high moor.

KNOT (Calidris canutus) [RW], [P]

J F M A M **J J A S** O N D

Small numbers recorded each year of this scarce passage migrant, with individuals occasionally overwintering. Up to 20 have wintered at

Dunster, but in recent years most records from September when numbers usually less than ten at Dunster and less than three at Porlock.

SANDERLING (Clidris alba) [P], [W]

J	F	M	A	**M**	J	J	**A**	**S**	**O**	**N**	**D**

Regular along the coast, usually in numbers of less than 20. Formerly up to 40 wintered at Dunster Beach but since the mid 1970s much rarer in December/January. Passage numbers at Dunster Beach usually less than five with smaller numbers at Porlock Marsh, so 60 at Dunster Beach on January 20th 1990 was exceptional.

LITTLE STINT (Calidris minuta) [P]

J	F	M	A	**M**	J	J	**A**	**S**	**O**	N	D

Rare passage migrant along Exmoor's coast. Recorded from Minehead Beach, Dunster Beach and Porlock Marsh. Numbers higher at Porlock Marsh where numbers of up to five are recorded in most years.

One winter record from Dunster Beach, January 9th 1949.

TEMMINK'S STINT (Calidris temminckii) [V]

J F M A M J J A Ⓢ O N D

One record of a single bird on Porlock Marsh, September 13th 1972.

BAIRD'S SANDPIPER (Calidris bairdii) [V]

J F M A M J J A Ⓢ O N D

One record of this North American wader of a single at Porlock Marsh, September 17th 1973. Another one was claimed at the same place on September 9th 1979, but was rejected by the British Birds Rarities Committee.

Baird's Sandpiper

61

PECTORAL SANDPIPER (Calidris melanotos) [V]

J	F	M	A	M	J	J	A	S	O	N	D

Four records of this transatlantic vagrant, three at Porlock Marsh (September 6th - October 13th 1947; September 19th - October 7th 1950; and more unusually in spring, May 5th 1974) and one at Minehead (September 8th - 16th 1954).

CURLEW SANDPIPER (Calidris Perruginea) [P]

J	F	M	A	M	J	J	**A**	**S**	**O**	N	D

Rare passage migrant with up to three recorded at either Porlock Marsh or Minehead/Dunster Beaches most years. There is one old record for Lynmouth also.

PURPLE SANDPIPER (Calidris maritima) [W]

J	**F**	M	A	M	J	J	A	S	**O**	**N**	**D**

Uncommon winter visitor with four to five along the coast from Woody Bay to Heddon's Mouth. Rare elsewhere although there are records from Dunster Beach — the most recent being of one on October 7th 1989. Away from Woody Bay to Heddon's Mouth usually ones and twos, although four were present at Dunster Beach on January 27th 1937.

DUNLIN (Calidris alpina) [RB], [P], [W]

J F M A M J J A S O N D

Recorded on the beaches most months of the year with peak numbers in winter. Bred on Exmoor in the late 1800s and pairs were seen displaying on a couple of occasions in the 1930s. However, there are no recent records of breeding. Small passage numbers at Wimbleball, with wintering numbers on the beaches rarely exceeding 200 at Dunster Beach and 100 at Porlock Marsh, although 239 present Dunster Beach, January 17th 1990.

Dunlin

RUFF (Philomachus pugnax) [P], [RW]

J F **M A M J J A S O** N D

One or two recorded most years on passage (mostly autumn) at Porlock Marsh, Dunster Beach and Wimbleball. Occasionally seen in winter, with one at Dunster Beach, February 3rd 1990. Exceptional was the record of 15 present at Porlock Marsh on April 15th - 17th 1987 with seven remaining until the 18th.

JACK SNIPE (Lymnocryptes minimus) [W]

J F M **A M J J A S** O **N D**

A scarce but regular visitor to Exmoor with most records from Porlock Marsh and Wimbleball. Numbers usually singles or occasionally pairs, although up to 15 were seen at Dunster before 1970 but not since.

SNIPE (Gallinago gallinago) [W], [B], [R]

J F M A M J J A S O N D

Small numbers breed regularly on Exmoor in upland marshy areas with up to 20 pairs in 1978. Also bred at Dulverton in 1931. Winter visitors swell resident numbers with up to 40 on the Chains, Brendons and coastal marshes. In the past up to 250 have been recorded at

Minehead Marshes in winter, but not since large areas of the marshes were drained for the building of the Butlin's holiday camp.

Snipe

GREAT SNIPE (Gallinago media) [V]

```
J  F  M  A  M  J  J  A  Ⓢ  O  N  D
```

A solitary old (and unauthenticated) record of one shot at Warren Ridge, September 22nd 1903.

LONG-BILLED DOWITCHER
(Limnodromus scolopaceus) [V]

J F M A M J J A S O N D

One record of this North American species, a single bird at Porlock Marsh, September 29th - October 26th 1973.

WOODCOCK (Scolopax rusticola) [RB], [RR], [W]

J F M A M J J A S O N D

Has bred in the past at Dunster (1922-23, 1945 and 1948), and at Cornham Farm, Simonsbath (1959). Since then there have been some summer records from Exmoor but it is now probably only a rare breeder, the most recent evidence of breeding being July 1981 when an adult and three young were at Bridgetown.

Most records are of winter birds with widespread records from scattered sites in most years, but fairly regularly at Wimbleball, and the Alcombe, Minehead and Porlock areas of Exmoor.

BLACK-TAILED GODWIT (Limosa limosa) [P]

J F M A M J J A S O N D

Rare autumn passage migrant, less frequent than Bar-tailed Godwit. Usually only records of singles from Minehead/Dunster beaches or from Porlock Marsh, although larger numbers are occasionally recorded, such as the eight present at Dunster Beach, September 4th 1987.

BAR-TAILED GODWIT (Limosa lapponica)   [P], [RW]

J	F	**M**	**A**	**M**	J	J	**A**	**S**	**O**	N	D

More frequent passage migrant than Black-tailed Godwit with occasional birds overwintering. Flocks of up to ten birds not infrequent in autumn at Dunster Beach with singles or pairs at Porlock Marsh. Larger numbers do occur however, with 26 at Dunster Beach, August 30th 1978 and 23 September 15th 1988. Ten at Porlock Marsh on May 5th 1989 was an unusually high number for there.

WHIMBREL (Numerius phaeopus)   [P], [RW]

J	F	M	**A**	**M**	J	J	**A**	**S**	O	N	D

A regular spring and autumn passage migrant, being fairly common along the coast and at Wimbleball. Numbers higher at Porlock Marsh with largest numbers on spring passage where up to 50 regular, and 92 there on April 30th 1988. Spring passage numbers at Dunster Beach up to ten. Numbers on autumn passage smaller with only small parties or individual birds present.

There is one winter record from Minehead, December 26th 1927.

67

CURLEW (Numenius arquata)   [B], [R], [P], [W]

| J | F | M | A | M | J | J | A | S | O | N | D |

Common along the coast most months of the year with peak numbers on autumn passage and over the winter period. A small number breed on the high moor each year although in smaller numbers than 1978 when up to 35 pairs bred. Autumn/winter numbers at Dunster/Minehead beaches up to 260, with up to 170 at Porlock.

One with a very short bill (about half normal length) present at Dunster Beach during the winter since November 1987, also being seen in July 1990.

SPOTTED REDSHANK (Tringa erythropus)   [RP], [RW]

| J | F | M | A | M | J | J | A | S | O | N | D |

Scarce passage migrant and occasional winter visitor, to the coast usually, although one was present at Wimbleball, August 1981. Less than annual with most recent records all from Porlock Marsh (November 1st and December 23rd 1986, and March 18th 1987)

REDSHANK (Tringa totanus)   [R], [B]

| J | F | M | A | M | J | J | A | S | O | N | D |

Regular along the coast and at Wimbleball, but never in large numbers. Up to four pairs breed most years at Porlock Marsh. Elsewhere numbers rarely exceed ten, usually less than that with up to four being the highest numbers in recent years.

GREENSHANK (Tringo nebularia) [P]

J	F	M	**A**	**M**	J	**J**	**A**	**S**	O	N	D

Scarce but regular passage migrant along the coast and at Wimbleball, with a few records from the high moor. Records from Minehead/Dunster Beaches, Porlock Marsh and Wimbleball usually concern single birds with three at Porlock Marsh, May 5th 1989, unusual.

GREEN SANDPIPER (Tringa ochropus) [P]

J	F	M	**A**	**M**	J	**J**	**A**	**S**	O	N	D

Regular passage records (especially autumn passage) from Wimbleball, (with numbers up to six) and, Porlock Marsh and Dunster Beach (usually singles or pairs). Also recorded from Chetsford Water, Goathill Bridge, Nutscale Reservoir and the beach at Glenthorne, (where four were present April 28th 1987).

WOOD SANDPIPER (Tringa glareola) [P]

J F M A Ⅿ J <u>J</u> <u>A</u> Ⓢ O N D

Less common passage migrant than Green Sandpiper, being very rare in spring with one record (at Minehead Marsh, May 26th - 28th 1955). Recorded from Wimbleball and also the coastal marshes, usually singly, but six were present at Porlock Marsh, July 30th 1972 and up to four at Wimbleball, August 28th 1978. The most recent record is of one at Porlock Marsh, August 16th 1986.

TEREK SANDPIPER (Xenus cinereus) [V]

J F M A Ⅿ J J A S O N D

One record of a single bird at Porlock Marsh, May 28th 1987.

Terek Sandpiper

COMMON SANDPIPER (Actitis hypoleucos)
[RB], [RW], [P]

J F M **A M** J **J A S O** N D

Bred on Exmoor, regularly until the 1920s on the Rivers Barle and Exe, and possibly since, though not recently. Fairly frequent passage migrant along the coast, streams and at Wimbleball with numbers up to ten at any location (with higher numbers recorded such as up to 16 at Wimbleball July - September 1989).

Occasionally overwinters — the most recent record being in 1988 with one at Minehead on January 13th.

TURNSTONE (Arenaria interpres) [P], [W]

J F M A M J J **A S O N D**

Seen most months on the coast, but rarely elsewhere. Autumn passage flocks of up to 250 have been recorded at Dunster Beach although numbers in recent years have been smaller. Flocks in winter have reached 100 in the past but in recent years rarely exceed 50. Spring passage numbers have reached 130 (Dunster Beach, April 13th 1962), but usually well below 100.

RED-NECKED PHALAROPE (Phalaropus lobatus) [V]

J	F	M	A	M	J	J	A	Ⓢ	Ⓞ	N	D

Only four records of this species, all of single birds:

- Porlock Marsh, September 26th 1957
- Porlock Marsh, October 11th - 12th 1961
- Porlock Marsh, September 28th 1969
- Porlock Weir, September 13th 1970.

Red-necked Phalarope

GREY PHALAROPE (Phalaropus fulicarius) [RP], [V]

J	F	M	A	M	J	J	A	S	O	N	D

Rare passage migrant or storm blown vagrant, usually after south-westerly gales. Seven records from Porlock and eight from Minehead, (one of a dead bird).

Porlock Marsh — one September 21st 1960; one November 2nd - 3rd 1967; one October 4th 1969; one September 8th 1974; two October 20th-26th 1984; one October 8th 1987.

Minehead — three November 10th 1959; one dead December 25th 1967; one December 23rd 1967; one October 14th-24th 1968; one September 28th 1969; one September 1st 1985.

POMARINE SKUA (Stercorarius pomarinus) [V]

J	F	M	A	M	J	J	A	S	O	N	D

Very rare storm vagrant with hardly any Exmoor records. A primary feather was found on Minehead Golf Course, April 18th 1947. Usually only single birds recorded but on October 16th 1886 twelve were seen off Minehead, and November 10th 1985 when 33 were seen flying west off Dunster Beach. More recently, two flew west off Dunster Beach on August 18th 1992.

ARCTIC SKUA (Stercorarius parasiticus) [P]

J F M A M̲ J J A̲ S̲ O N D

Scarce passage migrant. The most frequently recorded skua off the Exmoor coast with almost annual records, usually of singles, although small parties are occasionally seen. The majority of records are from Minehead/Dunster with others from Porlock and Glenthorne.

LONG-TAILED SKUA (Stercorarius longicaudus) [V]

J F M A Ⓜ J J A Ⓢ O N D

Vagrant. Two records:
- one at Minehead Golf Course, May 2nd - 4th 1947
- one off Dunster Beach, September 30th 1991.

GREAT SKUA (Stercorarius skua) [P]

J F M A M J̲ J̲ A S̲ O̲ N D

Rare passage migrant with singles regularly, (though not frequently) off Minehead/Dunster. Occasionally pairs seen such as September 15th 1966 when two were off Minehead.

Most recent records of singles off Porlock Bay (July 27th - 29th 1986),

Ivystone Rock (September 21st 1986), Porlock Bay (June 10th 1989) and Dunster Beach (October 7th 1989).

MEDITERRANEAN GULL (Larus melanocephalus)
[RP], [W]

J F M A M J J A S O N D

Scarce passage migrant and winter visitor, but annual. First recorded at Dunster Beach, December 31st 1956 (which was also the first Somerset record). What was probably the same bird returned September 23rd 1957.

Up to 1986 there were seven records from Dunster Beach. Since 1986 there have been 15 records (six of adults, seven of second year birds). There have been three records from Wimbleball, two of one flying over Minehead, and one from Porlock Weir. Usually singles although two or three have been seen together at Dunster Beach.

Mediterranean Gull and Black-headed Gull

LAUGHING GULL (Larus atricilla) [V]

```
J  F  M  A  M  J  J  A  S  O  N  D
```

One record of the North American Gull, a second winter bird at
Bossington Beach and Porlock Marsh, September 8th - 10th 1980.

LITTLE GULL (Larus minutus) [RP], [RW]

```
J  F  M  A  M  J  J  A  S  O  N  D
```

Rare passage migrant and winter storm blown vagrant, from the coast
(most recent records from Dunster Beach). Has been recorded inland,
with one found dying on a mill pond at Wootton Courtenay,
September 2nd 1982. Probably overlooked with many birds going
unrecorded.

SABINE'S GULL (Larus sabini) [V]

```
J  F  M  A  M  J  J  A  S  O  N  D
```

Four records of this species usually associated with strong winds:

- one spring record, an adult at Porlock Marsh, May
  30th to June 3rd 1953
- one Minehead/Dunster Beach, September 25th-
  26th 1986

76

- one juvenile in Porlock Bay, September 6th 1985
- one juvenile in Porlock Bay, August 12th 1989 (a very early date).

BLACK-HEADED GULL (Larus ridibundus)   [R], [W]

```
J F M A M J J A S O N D
```

Common all year with highest numbers in autumn and spring when large numbers occur on the shore, marshes, fields and built-up areas. May have bred in the past but no confirmed breeding records, although a pair were present at Porlock Marsh in late May 1974. Two night roosts are used: a small one at Porlock Marsh and one at Dunster Beach with between 1,000 and 1,800 birds.

RING-BILLED GULL (Larus delawarensis)   [V]

```
J F M A M J J A S O N D
```

One record of a first year bird at Dunster Beach, April 22nd 1991

COMMON GULL (Larus canus)   [P], [W]

```
J F M A M J J A S O N D
```

Regular winter visitor and passage migrant. The night time roost at Dunster Beach holds between 1,000 and 3,000 birds in winter with numbers at Wimbleball at this time up to 200. Has been seen passing offshore in large numbers also, such as the 300 flying south on January 28th 1988 off Dunster Beach. Uncommon on the high moor.

LESSER BLACK-BACKED GULL
(Larus fuscus) [B], [R], [W]
British Race (Larus fuscus graellsii)

```
J F M A M J J A S O N D
```

A few pairs bred on Martinhoe Cliffs up to 1984 and probably since. Non-breeding birds seen at Porlock, Wimbleball and Dunster Beach (with up to 20 wintering at the latter). Scarce most of the year with numbers usually less than ten.

North Scandinavian Race (Larus fuscus fuscus)

Vagrant. One old record - of a flock of about 30 flying off Glenthorne late March 1956 or 1957. Otherwise very rare with the most recent record of one at Hurlstone Point, July 30th 1989.

ICELAND GULL (Larus glaucordes)   [V]

```
J F M A M J J A S O N D
```

Vagrant. Five records:
- one second year Dunster Beach, January 26th-28th 1957

- one Minehead Seafront, January 8th 1971
- one Porlock Weir, December 26th 1989
- one Dunster Beach, February 1st-3rd 1990
- one Porlock Marsh, April 25th-May 7th 1991.

Lesser Black-backed Gull

GLAUCOUS GULL (Larus hyperboreus) [V]

Vagrant. Three records:
- one second winter Minehead December 24th - 30th 1968
- one at Dunster Beach, January 26th/27th 1991

- one at Porlock Marsh, April 26th-May 4th 1991, (present at the same time as an Iceland Gull which was unusual).

_____

HERRING GULL (Larus argentatus) [R], [B], [W]

J	F	M	A	M	J	J	A	S	O	N	D

During the 1970s some 400-500 pairs nested along the coast from Minehead to Combe Martin. However, numbers in recent years have rapidly declined with about 150 pairs in the early 1980s and now fewer than 50 pairs. Outside the breeding season numbers up to 200 in Porlock Bay/Marsh, up to 130 at Lynmouth and up to 100 on Minehead Beach. Up to 3,000 have been present at Minehead Beach in autumn (1954 and 1968). There are few records of migratory movements although 300 flew north east at Porlock Bay, April 11th 1966 and 150 flew west in 15 minutes off Minehead, December 27th 1966.

_____

GREAT BLACK-BACKED GULL (Larus marinus) [B], [R]

J	F	M	A	M	J	J	A	S	O	N	D

Breeds regularly along the coast, but usually in Devon-Exmoor (where two pairs usually breed), with pairs at Foreland, Lee Bay and Lynmouth quite often. Has bred also at Culbone (1968), and possibly Hurlstone Point. A few non-breeding birds usually present along the coast all year. Numbers in winter up to 15 at Dunster Beach roost. Also recorded from Wimbleball though in no great numbers.

_____

KITTIWAKE (Rissa tridactyla) [B], [R], [W], [P]

| J | F | M | A | M | J | J | A | S | O | N | D |

The first Exmoor breeding record was of six pairs on Martinhoe cliffs in 1972. Numbers increased up to 1984 when there were about 200 pairs. Since then a decline seems to have occurred with 220 occupied nests in 1987, 145 pairs in 1988, 60 breeding pairs in 1989 and 133 nests but no sign of any young in 1990. However in 1991 145 nests were present, and in 1992 200 pairs were present with about 100 pairs rearing young.

Coastal movements are regular, usually in strong north-west winds after south-westerly gales, and can involve very large numbers such as 4,000 - 5,000, December 21st 1982, and 'probably several thousand' west on December 24th 1984. Some records are unconnected with weather conditions however such as 85 passing north west off Dunster on September 2nd 1963.

SANDWICH TERN (Sterna sandvicensis) [P]

| J | F | **M** | **A** | **M** | J | J | **A** | **S** | **O** | N | D |

Scarce passage migrant, recorded most years in small numbers, usually singles or pairs, but up to ten. Most records from Dunster/Minehead Beaches, Porlock and Glenthorne. The maximum number recorded in spring is 22 on the shore at Minehead/Porlock, April 12th 1966. The highest number for autumn is 56 at Dunster Beach, August 20th 1983.

Sandwich Tern

ROSEATE TERN (Sterna dougallii) [V]

J F M A M J J A S O N D

The only Exmoor records of this species are of three on the beach at
Minehead, August 14th 1971 and again August 23rd 1971.

COMMON TERN (Sterna hirundo)
ARCTIC TERN (Sterna paradisaea) [P]

| J | F | M | A | M | J | J A S | O | N | D |

These two species are treated together because of the difficulties of specific identification, especially when flying offshore at a distance. Both are uncommon passage migrants being more common in autumn than in spring. Of those specifically identified, Common Terns are more frequent. Parties of up to 20 are regular with up to 50 not entirely unusual. There have been nine autumn counts of between 50 and 100 on the coast between Dunster and Porlock. Not all records are of birds flying past, with 19 Common Terns resting on Minehead Beach, September 5th 1988.

LITTLE TERN (Sterna albifrons) [P]

| J | F | M | A | M | J | J | A S | O | N | D |

Uncommon passage migrant, usually in autumn, and with most records from Minehead/Dunster and Porlock Beaches. More common at Minehead/Dunster than at Porlock with numbers usually less than five, so 25 at Minehead on August 20th 1948 was exceptional and, more recently, eight resting on the mud on Minehead Beach on July 31st 1992 was unusual.

BLACK TERN (Childonias niger) [P]

J F M A M J J A S O N D

Rare passage migrant — usually in fairly small numbers along the coast and also at Wimbleball where five were seen in May 1989. Numbers from the coast small with the most recent record being on Minehead Beach, where three adults were present, resting with Common Terns, on August 8th 1992.

WHITE-WINGED BLACK TERN
(Childonias leucopterus) [V]

J F M A M J J A S O N D

One record of this species - at Porlock Marsh, August 11th 1986.

GUILLIMOT (Uria aalge) [B], [P], [RW]

J F M A M J J A S O N D

Breeds in the Woody Bay area where there were 549 birds in 1987. Elsewhere a scarce visitor usually after storms in singles or pairs, although small parties of less than 20 are seen mainly between Porlock and Glenthorne in summer. Not many records from winter, but 40 auks flew west off Minehead on December 21st 1985, five of which

Guillimot

were definitely Guillimots, suggesting the species is under-recorded in winter.

RAZORBILL (Alca torda) [B], [P], RW]

| J | F | M | **A** | **M** | **J** | **J** | A | S | O | N | D |

Breeds at Woody Bay with 474 birds in 1988, and 400 in 1992; most just east of Highveer, but some at Ruddy Ball and Wringcliff, and a few at Foreland Point. West of Dunster small parties, or more usually singles, occasionally seen outside the breeding season, especially after winter storms.

BLACK GUILLIMOT (Cepphus grylle) [V]

| J | F | M | A | M | J | J | A | S | O | N | D |

Only two records of this species:
- four flying west off Dunster Beach, February 7th 1954
- one at Dunster Beach, August 25th 1991.

LITTLE AUK (Alle alle) [V]

J F M **A M J J A S O** N D

Rare storm vagrant. Records of exhausted individuals come from Minehead and Porlock Beaches, and also inland at Exford, Winsford and Porlock Vale. Most recently recorded in 1991 when one was seen well out off Minehead on November 22nd, and one was seen from Greenaleigh Point on November 25th.

PUFFIN (Fratercula arctica) [V]

J F M A M J J A S O **N D**

Storm vagrant. Before 1900 was seen off Minehead and Porlock from a summer cruise. Since then there have been the following records:

- 12 off Minehead, August 10th 1951
- one off Minehead, September 22nd 1965
- three off Minehead, October 3rd 1965
- one off Hurlstone Point, September 6th 1967
- one off Woody Bay, June 1970 (breeding plumage)
- two off Glenthorne, July 4th 1976

- one juvenile found at Warren Point, Minehead, August 20th 1976, later released off Minehead
- one off Porlock Weir, May 13th 1989.

FERAL PIGEON (ROCK DOVE) (Colombia livia) [B], [R]

J F M A M J J A S O N D

Unlikely to have occurred in its wild state (i.e. Rock Dove). Feral birds are found in small parties on the beaches, and in a number of towns on Exmoor, with up to 100 around Minehead.

STOCK DOVE (Columba oenas) [B], [R]

J F M A M J J A S O N D

Widely distributed and fairly common, nesting in woods and (more commonly on Exmoor) cattle sheds, barns and deserted buildings. In winter more likely to be found on arable land where about 250 were present at Dunster in December 1957. More recently 170 were near Luccombe, January/February 1989.

WOOD PIGEON (Columba palumbus) [B], [R]

J F M A M J J A S O N D

Common. An abundant breeding bird with large flocks in winter, when it is usually absent from open moorland. Breeds in bushes on the high moor, however. Some evidence of passage movements with 25 birds flying north, December 17th 1988 at Hurlstone Point, and 35 flew in off the sea at Hurlstone Point on November 8th 1986 having presumably just flown across from Wales.

COLLARED DOVE (Streptopelia decaocto) [R], [B]

| J | F | M | A | M | J | J | A | S | O | N | D |

Fairly common resident and passage migrant. The first record was one at Minehead on May 18th 1963, followed by a pair at Porlock. Since then, in common with other parts of the country, numbers have increased. Common around towns and village, but less so on higher ground. Winter flocks often up to 30 birds with 50 being seen on wires near Dunster, September 1983.

TURTLE DOVE (Streptopelia turtur) [S], [B], [P]

| J | F | M | A | M | J | J | A | S | O | N | D |

Scarce and local summer visitor and passage migrant. A few records each year, usually in the Minehead/Dunster and Brendons areas. Rare or absent in the Exmoor wooded valleys. Recent records of singles or pairs from Blackford (near Luccombe), Woodcombe, Wootton Courtenay, Dunster Beach, Bratton and Hopcott. One unusual record of a flock of 14 near Porlock on May 11th 1926 has not been equalled in recent years.

CUCKOO (Cuculus canorus) [B], [S]

| J | F | M | **A** | **M** | **J** | **J** | **A** | Ⓢ | O | N | D |

Common summer visitor to open woodland areas and also to moorland slopes. Meadow Pipits are the main host species (with Tree Pipit also common foster parents). In 1990 first seen and heard on April 1st which is exceptionally early, most arriving from mid-April onwards. Heard from 30-40 sites each year usually.

Cuckoo

BARN OWL (Tyto alba) [R], [RB]

J F M A M J J **A S O N D**

Has recently seen a serious decline with now only a handful of records each year, most from the winter period. Disappeared from parts of North Exmoor about 40 years ago in the early 1950s. Has bred in the past (at Dunster, Exford, Simonsbath, Challacombe, Minehead, Porlock and Monksilver), and reportedly bred near Lanacre in 1991 when six young were raised.

SNOWY OWL (Nyctea scandiaca) [V]

J F M **A M J J A S** O N D

Vagrant. At least four records, all of single birds:

- Exmoor Forest, March 22nd 1876
- various places between Haddon Hill and Dunster, October 12th 1925 - March 15th 1926
- Haddon Hill, January 18th 1930 (one also reported there in 1927 but no date or details)
- near Simonsbath, January 26th 1945.

There have been no recent records from Exmoor, though one at North Molton on March 9th 1972 was close.

LITTLE OWL (Athene noctua) [B], [R]

| J | F | M | A | M | J | J | A | S | O | N | D |

Not common anywhere, and absent from most of the valleys, but scattered breeding records, and a handful of out of breeding season sightings each year. Following the introduction of this species by Lord Lilford into the Midlands, it reached Dunster in 1914 and Dulverton by 1917. Most records concern singles but occasionally pairs.

TAWNY OWL (Strix aluco) [B], [R]

| J | F | M | A | M | J | J | A | S | O | N | D |

Widespread in woods and farmland where breeding occurs. Reported from 21 sites during 1990 with several records of pairs. Occasionally heard calling during the day, as in one heard calling at Wimbleball at 14.00 G.M.T. on January 2nd 1989.

LONG-EARED OWL (Asio otus) [V], [RB]

| J | F | M | A | M | J | J | A | S | O | N | D |

Very rare, but has bred in the past:

- 'Exmoor', 1942
- Winsford, 1968.

May also have nested at Horner before 1918. Also reported to have nested on the outskirts of Exmoor in 1989.

Winter records also from Minehead, Dunster, Porlock and Monksilver but none recently.

Long-eared Owl

SHORT-EARED OWL (Asio flammeus) [RB], [W]

J F M A M J J A S O **N D**

Regular winter visitor in small numbers. Has bred in the past - at Exford Common in 1939. Recent winter records from Stoke Pero Ridge, Haddon Hill, Valley of Rocks and Minehead Golf Course. Usually only one or two records per winter (less than annually) of single birds.

NIGHTJAR (Caprimulagus europaeus) [S], [B]

J	F	M	A	**M**	**J**	**J**	**A**	S	O	N	D

Breeds regularly on high ground, with the characteristic 'churring' heard in some cleared woodland, and on moorland fringes, from Alcombe Common to North Hill. There is one unusual record of breeding on the shingle at Porlock Beach.

SWIFT (Apus apus) [B], [S], [P]

J	F	M	A	**M**	**J**	**J**	**A**	S	O	N	D

Common summer visitor and passage migrant. Breeds in many old buildings and church towers. Feeding flocks regularly occur over the high moor, and can be quite large.

ALPINE SWIFT (Apus melba) [V]

J	F	M	A	M	J	J	A	S	O	N	D

Alpine Swift

Vagrant. Three records of this species:
- one at Porlock Marsh, October 5th 1954
- one at Minehead, April 22nd 1964
- one at Dunkery Beacon, May 27th 1980.

KINGFISHER (Alcedo atthis) [R], [B]

Nested on the River Avill in 1981 and often near Winsford, also on the River Exe and possibly the River Barle. Often rears two broods. In winter it visits coastal marshes and reservoirs more, and also a variety of other locations. Records fairly frequent, usually of singles and pairs.

Kingfisher

HOOPOE (Upupa epops) [RP]

| J | F | M | A | M | J | J | A | S | O | N | D |

Rare passage migrant in spring and autumn, being much less frequent in autumn. Since 1956 there have been 12 spring records and two autumn records, the most recent being of two on the coast path beyond Selworthy Beacon, September 22nd 1989.

Hoopoe

WRYNECK (Jynx torquilla) [RP]

| J F M A M J J A Ⓢ ◎ N D |

Rare autumn passage migrant, with the most recent records being:

- one at Dulverton, September 14th 1975
- one at North Hill, September 24th 1979
- one at Porlock, October 2nd 1989.

GREEN WOODPECKER (Picus viridis) [R], [B]

| **J F M A M J J A S O N D** |

Common resident, nesting from sea level up to the higher ground, (nested at 380m in the Barle Valley in 1977). Widespread breeder with juveniles reported from a wide variety of locations.

GREAT SPOTTED WOODPECKER
(Dendrocopos major) [R], [B]

| **J F M A M J J A S O N D** |

Resident, with some evidence of passage migration, as it has been observed flying west over the Exmoor plateau. Common breeder, although scarce in the higher woodland. In winter it disperses and tends to be a more common visitor to parks and gardens. Nests and young recorded from many sites.

Great Spotted Woodpecker

LESSER SPOTTED WOODPECKER
(Dendrocopos murior) [R], [B]

J F M A M J J A S O N D

Resident and scarce. Breeds in deciduous woods (including Horner and Selworthy) and also in the higher woods, where it has bred near the tree limit on the slopes of Dunkery. In winter tends to join wandering Tit flocks, and so records are more scattered and fairly frequent - possibly because the birds are more easily seen, with records from Horner, Great Haddon, Porlock, Alcombe and Minehead.

WOODLARK (Lullula arborea) [RW], [RP], [RB]

J F M A M J J A S O N D

Rare passage migrant and winter visitor. Has bred. Nested around Porlock to Dunster until 1946. Hard winters in 1946 and 1962 wiped out the local population. Occasional records in the breeding season have also come from Oare, Winsford and Dulverton.

Since then only scattered records, mainly of winter birds. A wintering record is of five at Lynch near Porlock, January 23rd - February 6th 1976. The most recent record is of a singing male at Haddon Hill, June 20th 1986.

SKYLARK (Alanda arvensis) [R], [B]

J F M A M J J A S O N D

A common and widespread breeder on Exmoor, apparently with a breeding density higher than the national average. In winter tends to come down from the high moor (with the high moor largely deserted from October/November to March), and form flocks on the coast and nearby fields, reaching numbers of up to several hundred in hard weather.

SHORELARK (Eremophila alpestris) [RW]

J F M A M J J A S O N D

Rare winter visitor. Up to 1970 only six records, three each from Minehead and Porlock Marsh, all singles:

- Minehead, spring 1911
- Minehead, October 29th 1915
- Minehead, December 25th 1939
- Porlock Marsh, November 2nd 1926
- Porlock Marsh, March 21st 1937
- Porlock Marsh, November 6th 1963.

Since then most records have been from Porlock, usually singles, but occasionally more, with 13 at Porlock, November 1st 1976 being exceptional. The most recent record is of one male at Porlock Marsh, October 27th 1988.

SAND MARTIN (Riparia riparia) [S], [P], [B]

J F **M A M J J** A S O N D

Breeding records from the River Barle between Simonsbath and Withypool; the River Exe near Exford and Dulverton, with odd breeding records of pairs at Wootton Courtenay and Porlock. Passage records from Wimbleball and the coast, when up to 40 occur regularly.

The breeding population was probably about 20 pairs (with fluctuations from year to year), but no nesting records after 1989, until 1992 when eight pairs bred on the River Exe near Exbridge on the National Park boundary.

SWALLOW (Hirundo rustica) [S], [B], [P]

Usually arrives at the end of March, so three at Porlock Marsh, March

J F **M A M** J J A **S O** N D

18th 1992 were quite early, with spring passage more noticeable than autumn. A widespread and common breeder. An exceptional record of three photographed in a barn in Minehead, January 20th 1975, had been seen at Selworthy the previous day. A pair were also seen building a nest at Minehead, January 24th 1975 and presumably involved two of these three.

RED-RUMPED SWALLOW (Hirundo daurica) [V]

J F M A M J J A S ◎ N D

One record of a single bird at Porlock, October 29th 1987, at the time when there was an influx of this species into Britain as a whole.

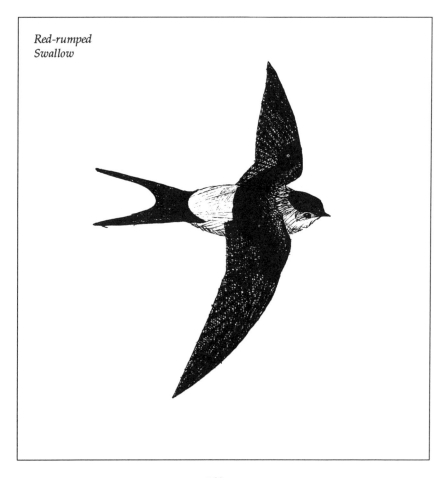

*Red-rumped
Swallow*

HOUSE MARTIN (Delichon urbica) [S], [B], [P]

| J | F | 𝕄 | **<u>A</u>** | **<u>M</u>** | **<u>J</u>** | **<u>J</u>** | **<u>A</u>** | **<u>S</u>** | **<u>O</u>** | N | 𝔻 |

Widespread breeder especially in towns, villages and also moorland farms. Of the three hirundines, House Martin is usually the last to arrive, with coastal passage being obvious. Often seen in large numbers, but 5,500 plus over Bossington and Porlock Marsh, October 4th 1987 was of note. There is an exceptionally late record of one at Minehead on Christmas Day 1974 and at Alcombe two days later.

RICHARD'S PIPIT (Anthus novaeseelandiae) [V]

| J | F | 𝕄 | A | M | J | J | A | S | ○ | ℕ | D |

Three records of single birds:
- one at Dunster, November 27th 1977
- one at Minehead, March 11th - 18th 1980
- one at Dunster Beach, October 30th 1991.

TAWNY PIPIT (Anthus campestris) [V]

| J | F | M | A | M | J | J | 𝔸 | S | O | N | D |

This species has only recently joined the Exmoor list with a moulting juvenile at Dunster Beach on August 4th 1993.

TREE PIPIT (Anthus trivialis)   [S], [B], [P]

J F M **A M J J A S** O N D

Fairly widespread on the moor and locally around Minehead, Dunster and the Brendons. Tends to favour the sunny hillsides, with at least 20 singing males reported most years.

MEADOW PIPIT (Anthus pratensis)   [B], [S], [R], [W], [P]

J F M A M J J A S O N D

Commonest (and often the only) passerine breeding on the higher moor. On passage and in winter common along the coast, but usually retreats from the high moor in severe winter weather. Passage numbers along the coast can often reach 40-50 at one time, with smaller numbers remaining to winter.

ROCK PIPIT (Anthus petrosus)   [R], [B], [W]

J F M A M J J A S O N D

Regular but scarce resident of coastal areas, with about 15-20 pairs breeding between Minehead and Heddon's Mouth. A handful of individuals winter along the coast, but rarely above five at any one location, at a time.

WATER PIPIT (Anthus spinoletta) [RP], [RW]

J F **M A M J J A S O** N D

Very rare passage migrant and winter visitor with only a handful of winter records, the most recent one being of one at Porlock Marsh, January 20th 1988.

_____

YELLOW WAGTAIL (Motacilla flava flavissima)
[S], [P], [RB]

J F M **A M J J A S** O N D

Regular spring and autumn passage migrant with most records from the coast although occasionally from Wimbleball. Has nested at Porlock Marsh, but is not a regular breeder. Passage numbers along the coast up to about 20 at Dunster Beach and 10 at Porlock Marsh, in spring; and small numbers in autumn when singles/pairs usual with occasionally small parties. One exceptionally late date of one at Porlock Marsh, November 13th 1989.

_____

Blue-headed Wagtail
(Motacilla flava flava) [S], [P], [RB]

Very rare passage migrant. Has bred. Twenty records at Minehead/ Porlock Marshes up to 1965, mainly singles or pairs, but three from Porlock Marsh, April 24th - 25th 1935. A handful of records since, most recently from Porlock Marsh, April 17th 1977.
Bred at Porlock Marsh 1951 and 1965 and probably 1956.

_____

GREY WAGTAIL (Motacilla cinerea) [R], [B]

```
J  F  M  A  M  J  J  A  S  O  N  D
```

Resident on most streams and rivers from the high moor (up to 420 m [1,400 feet]) to the coast. Nests in these areas and often near buildings, such as Selworthy Green, Bossington, Parks' Walk, and Periton Lane, Minehead.

Other breeding records from Hawkcombe, Badgworthy Water, Horner, Brushford, East Lyn (approximately five pairs between Malmsmead and Lynmouth), Chetsford Water and Wimbleball.

In winter disperses and found more commonly in the sheltered combes and on the coast.

PIED WAGTAIL (Motacilla alba yarrellii) [R], [B]

```
J  F  M  A  M  J  J  A  S  O  N  D
```

Common resident and passage migrant. Often breeds close to farms and houses, being scarce or absent above 250m. Passage most noticeable along the coastal areas where groups of up to 40 are regular in autumn. A flock of 60 at Dunster Beach, January 28th 1989 was fairly unusual.

White Wagtail (Motacilla alba alba)

Regular passage migrant along the coast mainly recorded in spring (probably because it is easier to separate from Pied Wagtail then). Largest numbers seen at Porlock Marsh with 33 present between April 15th-26th 1988 but flocks of less than 15-20 more usual.

White Wagtail

WAXWING (Bombycilla garrulus) [V]

J F M **A M J J A S O** N D

Rare and irregular winter visitor. Since 1967 there have been six records, two from Minehead, two from Alcombe, one from Dulverton and one from Brushford (Minehead, November 28th 1967 - January 1st 1968 and winter 1990; Alcombe, December 4th-6th 1975 and November 30th-December 4th 1976; Dulverton, January 22nd 1987 and Brushford, March 22nd 1987).

One at Dulverton, May 21st 1931 was perhaps an escapee, although spring records are not unheard of.

DIPPER (Cinclus cinclus) [R], [B]

J F M A M J J A S O N D

Common resident of the fast flowing streams on Exmoor, found from 500m down to sea level. About 75 pairs are estimated to be present on Exmoor. Has bred in almost all suitable habitats — including the Rivers Barle, Exe and Avill, Nutscale, Watersmeet, Wimbleball, Lynmouth, Horner Water and Badgworthy Water.

One male seen displaying to its mate on the East Lyn on November 22nd 1990 was unusual for winter.

Dipper

108

WREN (Troglodytes troglodytes) [R], [B]

J F M A M J J A S O N D

Common resident. Breeds anywhere with suitable cover, from sea level up to 500m in the combes. In winter often roosts in company and nestboxes can hold quite a few (up to 20), keeping warm together.

DUNNOCK (Prunella modularis) [R], [B]

J F M A M J J A S O N D

A common resident, especially in woodland areas with dense undergrowth, hedgerows, coastal scrub and gardens. Scarce in exposed moorland areas. Some vertical migration occurs since many leave the Exmoor combes in winter.

ROBIN (Erithacus rubecula) [R], [B], [W]

J F M A M J J A S O N D

Very common resident, absent only above the upper limit of bushes on exposed hilltops. Prefers open woodland, hedgerows, parks and gardens. In autumn/winter resident numbers are increased by migrants from the north and east.

NIGHTINGALE (Luscinia megarhynchos)   [RB], [RS]

J F M A M J J A S O N D

Rarely heard singing in Exmoor now, although bred at Bossington up to about 1935-40 when apparently suitable habitat became deserted. Other breeding and summer records since 1940 from Dunster area, Timberscombe and Minehead. In the past few years single birds have been heard singing on North Hill, Conygar Woods (Dunster), Withycombe Hill and Dunster Beach.

Regularly heard just outside the National Park at Washford, Old Cleeve and Watchet.

BLACK REDSTART (Phoenicurus ochruros)   [P]

J F M A M J J A S O N D

Scarce passage migrant usually in November/December with up to five recorded most years. Most records are coastal although a few records from Wimbleball and also at other inland sites, such as the male at the ruined sheep fold at the top of Hoar Oak on October 17th 1992. Usually singles, but three present at Exford during the first week of November 1975 and one exceptional record of five at Simonsbath November 10th 1982.

Much less common in spring with the most recent being one at Malmsmead, May 19th 1989. One summer record of a male at Oare, July 6th 1978.

REDSTART (Phoenicurus phoenicurus) [S], [B], [P]

J F M <u>A M J J A S O</u> N D

Common summer visitor and passage migrant. Has increased in recent years as a breeding species. An estimated 40-60 pairs bred on Exmoor in 1987, but this may be an underestimate, as many wooded areas are rarely visited. Usually arrives in the second week in April with return passage from mid-July to mid-October. Passage is most noticeable on the coast where single birds are regularly seen.

WHINCHAT (Saxicola rubetra) [S], [B], [P]

J F Ⓜ <u>A M J J A S</u> ◎ N D

Whinchat

111

Common summer visitor and passage migrant. A 1978 survey suggested 450-600 pairs on Exmoor (about 1.5% of the UK population). However a survey in 1990 put the figure at only just over 100 pairs - showing a serious decline over the last 10-12 years.

The 1978 figures have been accused of being excessively high. Even so it still shows a serious decline in their numbers. Usually arrives from mid-April onwards — so one at Halse Combe, March 24th 1989 was exceptionally early. In autumn groups of up to five seen along the coast.

STONECHAT (Saxicola torquata) [R], [B]

J F M A M J J A S O N D

Widely distributed and locally common. A 1978 survey found up to 150 pairs on Exmoor, with a 1990 survey finding about 110 pairs therefore indicating that numbers have remained fairly steady in recent years. In winter tends to migrate from the higher moor to coastal areas.

WHEATEAR (Oenanthe oenanthe) [S], [B], [P]

J F M A M J J A S O N D

Fairly common breeder with 66 pairs found in a survey in 1989: the coast, Royal Forest area and Barle Valley having most nests, with areas like Badgworthy Water, Dunkery Barrows and Wimbleball Lake having been deserted since a survey in 1978 (which found about 100 breeding pairs). Nests in stone walls, ruined buildings and cavities among rocks (and once on Minehead Golf Course).

On passage parties of 10-15 regularly seen, especially on the coast; most birds arrive mid-March, (with one March 7th 1989 and a male, March 4th 1992, unusually early) and depart in October, singles occasionally remaining into November.

Greenland Wheatear (Oenanthe oenanthe leucorrhoa)

Small numbers of this larger, brighter race seen most years, mainly at Porlock Marsh. Most records in spring, probably because of not being so easy to identify when out of breeding plumage.

RING OUZEL (Turdus torquatus) [S], [B]

J	F	M	A	<u>M</u>	<u>J</u>	<u>J</u>	<u>A</u>	<u>S</u>	<u>O</u>	N	D

Scarce summer visitor with about 30 pairs breeding in the moorland combes from Dunkery to Hoar Oak, above 350m. On passage recorded along the coast but not regularly. Rare on Exmoor during late autumn, so five (probably a family) at Chalkwater, October 18th 1988 was unusual.

BLACKBIRD (Turdus merula) [R], [B], [P]

<u>J</u>	<u>F</u>	<u>M</u>	<u>A</u>	<u>M</u>	<u>J</u>	<u>J</u>	<u>A</u>	<u>S</u>	<u>O</u>	<u>N</u>	<u>D</u>

Common resident with some passage movement. Occurs in woodland, farmland, hedgerows, parks and gardens, even town centres. However few are found above 350m on the moor.

FIELDFARE (Turdus pilaris) [W], [P]

J F M Ⓐ **M J J A** Ⓢ **O N D**

Winter visitor and passage migrant with numbers fluctuating annually - depending on weather conditions on the continent and also on the abundance of food in Scandinavia.

Fieldfare form large roving flocks, often up to 200 and often mixed with Redwings. They usually arrive mid-October and leave mid-March. Passage migration is usually visible — such as the 700 an hour flying east at Dunster Beach, October 29th/30th 1988.

SONG THRUSH (Turdus philomelos) [R], [B], [W]

J F M A M J J A S O N D

Breeds in any habitat associated with trees, being a common resident and widespread breeder. In 1983 one pair even nested among heather on the slopes of Dunkery at 460m.

Local birds are joined by additional numbers in winter, some probably, of the greyer continental race Turdus philomelos.

REDWING (Turdus iliacus) [W], [P]

J F M Ⓐ **M J J A** Ⓢ **O N D**

Redwing

Regular winter visitor and passage migrant, usually more common than Fieldfares with which it associates. As with the Fieldfare, passage migration often visible, with about 550 an hour flying east over Dunster Beach area, October 29th/30th 1988.

MISTLE THRUSH (Turdus viscivorus) [RB], [RR]

J F M A M J J A S O N D

Common breeding resident, found in large gardens, woodlands, and moorland combes although absent on hilltops and open moorland.

After breeding, tend to form large roving flocks of up to 250 (although up to 40 more regular).

CETTI'S WARBLER (Cettia cetti) [RB], [RR]

J F M A M J J A S O N D

A very rare resident; has probably bred. The first record was of one at Dunster, November 27th 1976. A male was present all summer at Minehead in 1984, while breeding probably took place at Dunster in 1985. A singing male at Dunster in 1986 from May 12th-June 30th was probably one of a pair present there in January and February 1986. One was seen at Dunster Beach on January 4th 1991, and this species may be seen more regularly if it continues to expand its breeding range, as it has been doing in recent years.

GRASSHOPPER WARBLER (Locustella naevia) [S], [B], [P]

J F M **A M J J A** S O N D

Regular but scarce summer visitor and passage migrant. Nests in overgrown vegetation in marshes, heather moorland and young conifer plantations. Numbers fluctuate from year to year, with up to five heard/seen in recent years. Is probably under-recorded, however.

SEDGE WARBLER (Acrocephalus schoenobaenus)
[S], [B], [P]

J F M **A M J J A S** ◎ N D

Summer visitor and passage migrant. Has bred on Minehead and Porlock Marshes. Although no definite recent breeding records, singing males and pairs are seen at Minehead/Porlock Marshes and at the Somerwest World camp, every year in the breeding season. Regular on passage with records away from the coast at Wimbleball and Simonsbath.

Sedge Warbler

REED WARBLER (Acrocephalus scirpaceus) [S], [B], [P]

J F M <u>A M J J A S</u> ⦿ N D

Scarce summer visitor with most records from Minehead and Porlock Marshes, where a few pairs still breed. Pre-Butlin's used to breed at Minehead Clay Pits — though singing males and pairs still recorded from the camp. A few pairs present at Dunster Hawn where one pair certainly bred in 1991 and probably previously.

ICTERINE WARBLER (Hippolais icterina) [V]

J F M A M J J A S ⦿ N D

Vagrant. Two records:

- one in the Heddon Valley, October 7th 1972
- one at Withypool, August 17th 1975.

DARTFORD WARBLER (Sylvia undata) [V]

J F M A M J J A S ⦿ N D

Vagrant. Four records:

- one Bossington Hill, November 20th - 26th 1974
- one Bossington Hill, October 22nd 1976

118

- one North Hill (Minehead), December 6th 1982
- one (male) Heddon Valley, January 20th 1987.

Dartford Warbler

BARRED WARBLER (Sylvia nisoria) [V]

J F M A M J J A S O N D

Vagrant. One record, of an immature male at Porlock Marsh, August 8th 1969.

LESSER WHITETHROAT (Sylvia curruca) [S], [P], [RB]

J F M **A M J J A S** O N D

Very scarce summer visitor and passage migrant. Has bred in the Porlock Vale but no recent nesting records, although singing males heard on North Hill, Woodcombe and Bratton, in recent years.

WHITETHROAT (Sylvian communis) [S], [P], [B]

J F M **A M J J A S O** N D

Fairly common and widespread summer visitor. Breeds in hedgerows, woodland clearings, thickets, scrub and gorse, from sea level up to 500m where it breeds up to the limit of bushes in the combes. Numbers seem to be increasing from the figures of 1969 when they suffered a dramatic drop in population.

GARDEN WARBLER (Sylvia borun) [S], [P], [B]

J F M **A M J J A S** O N D

Fairly common summer visitor and passage migrant. Often occurs along the scrub in the moorland combes, such as Halse Combe and Cloutsham. Passage migrants often seen along the coast especially Dunster Beach and Porlock Marsh.

BLACKCAP (Sylvia atricapilla) [S], [P], [B], [RW], [RR]

J F **M A M J J A S** O N D

Summer visitor and passage migrant with some birds overwintering. Common from woodlands to parks and gardens. Overwintering birds seen at Porlock and Minehead where they frequently visit gardens.

Wintering birds number about six (Minehead/Alcombe) with singles or pairs from Dulverton, Bossington and Porlock.

YELLOW-BROWED WARBLER
(Phylloscopus inornatus) [V]

J F M A M J J A S O N D

Vagrant. Two records:

- one at Exford, April 11th 1970
- one at Dunster Hawn, March 11th-April 9th 1990.

Most UK records come from the autumn, with spring records very rare. However this species has been known to over-winter — and hence these records might refer to birds which arrived in autumn and overwintered, being overlooked until spring.

Yellow-browed Warbler

WOOD WARBLER (Phylloscopus sibilatrix) [S], [B], [P]

J F M **A M J J A S** O N D

Common in the oakwoods of Exmoor such as Horner Woods, Cloutsham Woods, Hawkcombe, Culbone, Hopcott, North Hill and Tivington. Usually arrives mid-April, so one at Dunster Hawn, April 2nd 1990 was quite early.

CHIFFCHAFF (Phylloscopus collybita)
[S], [P], [B], [RW], [RR]

J	F	**M**	**A**	**M**	**J**	**J**	**A**	**S**	**O**	N	D

Common summer visitor and passage migrant with a handful of birds overwintering. Breeds commonly in most woods, but avoids the comparatively treeless higher ground. On passage occurs almost anywhere even along Exmoor windbreaks miles from trees.

Overwintering birds mainly on the coast, with a few at Dunster Hawn, higher numbers (up to six or seven) at Porlock Marsh and singles elsewhere such as Wimbleball and Woodcombe. Out of seven at Porlock Marsh in winter periods of 1988/89 and 1989/90, at least five birds showed characteristics of the greyer eastern races P.c. abietinus (from Scandinavia) and P.c. Tortus (from Siberia).

WILLOW WARBLER
(Phylloscopus trochilus) [S], [B], [P], [RW], [RR]

J	F	**M**	**A**	**M**	**J**	**J**	**A**	**S**	O	N	D

Abundant summer visitor and passage migrant being more common and widespread than the Chiffchaff. Nests in any bushy growth including the moorland combes where it is the commonest warbler. One record of an overwintering bird at Dunster Beach, January 11th 1988.

GOLDCREST (Regulus regulus) [R], [B]

J F M A M J J A S O N D

Resident, and common, especially in conifer plantations, but frequent elsewhere in winter when it joins roving Tit flocks. Breeds in large gardens, woods, parks and even moorland combes. Severe winters can seriously affect Goldcrest numbers, as in 1979 and 1986.

FIRECREST (Regulus ignicapillus) [RP], [RW]

J F M A M J J A S O N D

Rare winter visitor and passage migrant. Up until 1966 about 15 records, mainly from Dunster and Porlock areas, with one on Exmoor. Usually singles, except three at Porlock Marsh January 16th-28th 1963. In recent years almost annual. Most winter records on the coast with as many as seven at Dunster, November-December 1982. One at Horner Water, May 31st 1973 may have been a prospective breeding bird while a singing male was at Monksilver, July 18th 1989. Recent winter sightings include two from Woodcombe (1987 and 1989) and one at Bossington 1988.

SPOTTED FLYCATCHER (Muscicapa striata) [S], [P], [B]

J F M A M J J A S O N D

Firecrest

Fairly common summer visitor and passage migrant, found in a variety of habitats from deciduous woodland to farms and gardens. Numbers are variable from year to year, and it may be absent from the Exmoor valleys some years. On passage often found on, or near the coast.

PIED FLYCATCHER (Ficedula hypoleuca)   [S], [P], [B]

J F M **A M** J J **A** S **O** N D

Summer visitor, common in woodland areas. Has bred on Exmoor regularly since the mid 1920s. Before 1970 less than 30 pairs but with the introduction of nestboxes from the late 1970s onwards numbers have greatly increased. In 1990, 148 boxes were put up, at Upton Cleeve (18), Farley Wood (12), Hawkcombe (30), Horner Woods (61), Treborough Woods (15) and Woodcock Gardens (12). Thirty-eight boxes were successfully used by Pied Flycatchers. Also breeds at Selworthy, Dunster and possibly Glenthorne.

BEARDED TIT (Panaurus biarmicus) [RP], [RW]

J F M A M J J A S ◎ Ⓝ Ⓓ

Very rare winter visitor/passage migrant. First record was of three at Porlock Marsh, October 28th 1972; since then only a handful of records, the most recent one being at Dunster Beach, October 11th 1990.

LONG-TAILED TIT (Aegithalos caudatus) [R], [B]

J F M A M J J A S O N D

Relatively common in woods, hedgerows and scrub. In autumn flocks of up to 50 common. There is one record of apparent migration with 12 coming in from the sea at Minehead, October 3rd 1954.

One record of a white headed bird showing characteristics of the race A.c. caudatus at Horner Woods, April 20th 1986.

MARSH TIT (Parus palustris) [R], [B]

J F M A M J J A S O N D

Resident - locally common. Found in old oak and ash woods, alders, willows, orchards and large gardens. More widespread in winter when often associated with mixed Tit flocks, but scarce on high and exposed ground. Breeds in Horner Woods, Woodcombe and Wheddon Cross among other places.

WILLOW TIT (Parus montanus) [R], [B]

J F M A M J J A S O N D

Scarce resident. Prefers damp birch, alder and willow woodlands. Only regularly recorded breeding at Wimbleball, but has bred at Brompton Regis, Alcombe Common and Dunster.

COAL TIT (Parus ater) [R], [B]

J F M A M J J A S O N D

Common resident in woods and gardens. On the Brendons is most numerous in conifer plantations, where it is the commonest breeding Tit. In winter more widely distributed as it joins foraging flocks of mixed Tits.

BLUE TIT (Parus caerulens) [B], [R]

J F M A M J J A S O N D

Blue Tit

Abundant and widespread resident, breeding in woods, gardens and
moorland combes.   In autumn and winter flocks also common in reed
beds and phragmites.   Breeds successfully in nestboxes with 66 pairs
successful out of the 148 boxes up in 1990 (see under Pied Flycatcher for
details).

GREAT TIT (Parus major) [R], [B]

J F M A M J J A S O N D

Very common resident in deciduous woods, gardens and hedges. In winter forms flocks (often with other Tits) and may be found anywhere. Out of the 148 nestboxes up in Exmoor woods (see under Pied Flycatcher for details), nine were successfully used by breeding pairs in 1990.

NUTHATCH (Sitta europaea) [R], [B]

J F M A M J J A S O N D

Common resident in mature deciduous woods and more widespread in winter when it joins Tit flocks and often visits bird tables. Has been seen up to 350m at places like Stoke Pero. In 1990 there were nine pairs which successfully bred in the 148 nestboxes set up in the various woods (see under Pied Flycatcher for details).

TREECREEPER (Certhia familiaris) [R], [B]

J F M A M J J A S O N D

Common resident — found in similar habitats to Nuthatch but more widespread, sometimes found in parks, gardens and occasionally conifer plantations. In winter often associates with Tit flocks. Numbers fluctuate according to the severity of winter weather.

GOLDEN ORIOLE (Oriolus oriulus) [RS], [RP]

```
J  F  M  A  M  J  J  A  S  O  N  D
```

Very rare summer visitor and passage migrant. There are a few spring records from Minehead, Dulverton, Woody Bay (May 2nd 1973), Dunster (at least two) and Horner Woods (May 23rd 1981). Most recent record is one at Withycombe 1986.

ISABELLINE SHRIKE (Lanius isabellinus) [V]

```
J  F  M  A  M  J  J  A  S  O  N  D
```

Only one record, of a first winter bird on Minehead Golf Course, September 22nd-24th 1989. This was the first Somerset record of this Asian species and attracted many observers.

RED-BACKED SHRIKE (Lanius collurio)
[V], [RS], [RP], [RB]

```
J  F  M  A  M  J  J  A  S  O  N  D
```

Vagrant. Formerly a summer visitor and passage migrant. Bred in the past, up until about 1962.
Only three records since:
                    - one at North Hill, August 19th 1973

- one at Bilbrook, May 22nd 1975
- one at Porlock Marsh, May 25th 1987 (was heard singing occasionally).

LESSER GREY SHRIKE (Lanius minor) [V]

| J | F | M | A | M | J | J | A | S | O | N | D |

One record - of one near Exford on April 8th 1967.

GREAT GREY SHRIKE (Lanius excubitor) [RW]

| J | F | M | A | M | J | J | A | S | O | N | D |

Great Grey Shrike

Rare winter visitor, recorded most years (usually single records of one bird), from a variety of locations including Winsford Hill, Croydon Hill, Chetsford, Porlock Allotment and Shallowford (near Lynton). Due to the surprising ease with which they can remain hidden, and the vast areas of under-watched moorland which are suitable, they are probably under-recorded.

One summer record of a single at Raleigh's Cross, April 26th-9th July 1953.

WOODCHAT SHRIKE (Lanius senator) [V]

J	F	M	A	M	J	J	A	S	O	N	D

One record - of one near Bossington, May 26th-27th 1926.

JAY (Garrulus glandarius) [R], [B], [RP]

J	F	M	A	M	J	J	A	S	O	N	D

Common resident of woodland areas. Usually seen in pairs or small family parties. Occasional passage migrant, such as in 1983 when there was a large influx into South West England. Flocks of 15-20 were seen flying east along the cliff top at Woody Bay and on November 3rd 1983 800 plus flew out to sea at the same place.

132

MAGPIE (Pica pica) [R], [B]

J F M A M J J A S O N D

Very common and widespread resident. Scarce on the high moor, although it does nest high up in the thorn bushes of isolated combes. Common in woodland, valleys, farmland, parks and gardens. In winter small flocks common of up to 10-15, though occasionally more.

NUTCRACKER (Nircifraga caryocatactes) [V]

J F M A M J J A S O N D

Vagrant. Four records of three (or possibly four) birds:

- one at Dunster, August/September 1940
- one at Wootton Courtenay, October 3rd-23rd 1968
- one at Minehead, October 27th 1968
- one at West Luccombe, August 10th 1985.

CHOUGH (Pyrrhocorax pyrrhocorax) [V], [RB]

Until 1869, when driven away by rock falls, bred on the cliffs west of Minehead. Bred until 1910 at Lynton cliffs and three juveniles were seen at Bossington in the summer of 1910, which may indicate breeding there, although they could have wandered away from Lynton.

In 1878 seven were seen near County Gate and one was present at Glenthorne 1910. One was at Hurlstone Point in the summer of 1919. Since then all records have been of single birds:

- Dunster, December 1923
- Porlock Weir, early 1929
- near Minehead, late December 1936- January 28th 1937
- Lynton, March 13th 1972
- North Hill, July 1973
- Lynmouth, April 20th 1980
- Valley of Rocks, September 30th 1989
- Foreland Point, September 28th 1990
- Horner Water, May 19th 1991, possibly the same one as above.
- Chalk Water, January 13th 1991
- Madacombe, January 13th 1991.

Chough

134

JACKDAW (Corvus monedula) [R], [B]

J	F	M	A	M	J	J	A	S	O	N	D

Very common. Breeds in colonies along coastal cliffs, quarries, old buildings, chimneys, parklands, woods and hedgerow trees. Large flocks of birds occur in fields as they feed by day, and then return to roost at dusk.

ROOK (Corvus frugilegus) [R], [B]

J	F	M	A	M	J	J	A	S	O	N	D

Common resident with most breeding in rookeries in tall hedgerows and trees close to human settlement. Most breed below 125m but there is a colony at Simonsbath at 400m. In autumn and winter large feeding flocks occur often running into hundreds. Albinos occur occasionally with a dull pink sandstone-coloured bird at Holdstone Down, March 31st 1987.

CARRION CROW (Corvus corone) [R], [B]

J	F	M	A	M	J	J	A	S	O	N	D

Common and widespread. Nests in trees, hedges and moorland combes. Nests have been found as low as 1m on isolated trees on the moor. Not usually associated with flocking as Jackdaws and Rooks are, but there was a large roost of 60 plus at Dunster Beach, December 26th 1978.

Hooded Crow (Corvus corone cornix)

Vagrant. A handful of records, mainly on the coast from Dunster to Porlock and mainly winter records. The most recent records are all of singles:

- Hawkcombe Head, January 1975
- Withiel Florey, September 4th 1975
- Dunster Beach, December 20th 1990 to March 2nd 1991.

RAVEN (Corvus corax) [R], [B]

J F M A M J J A S O N D

Resident and fairly common, with a number of ancestral breeding sites. Has recovered numbers well from the nineteenth century when only a few pairs existed. Now well distributed with breeding occasionally occurring in quarries in the Brendons. Large flocks seen occasionally, with flocks of up to 30 regular over moorland combes during autumn 1983. Two exceptional records, one of 107 feeding on a dead sheep, Farley Water, September 21st 1975 and one of 110 feeding on a dead sheep, March 1978.

STARLING (Sturnus vulgaris) [R], [B], [P]

J F M A M J J A S O N D

Abundant and widespread resident, breeding wherever buildings and trees provide suitable sites, although scarce or absent in the higher moorland valleys. Also a passage migrant, with migration noticeable on the coast where flocks of up to several thousand pass through the fields. Winter flocks can also contain large numbers with about 6,000 in the fields by Minehead Golf Course, February 1st 1990. Migration is also noted at Glenthorne in March and April with small flocks moving east.

ROSE-COLOURED STARLING (Sturnus roseus) [V]

J F M A Ⓜ Ⓙ Ⓙ A S O Ⓝ Ⓓ

Rose-coloured Starling

137

Four records, all of single birds:

- Porlock, July 25th 1945
- Porlock Marsh, May 14th 1957
- Wootton Courtenay, November 2nd 1975
- Dunster, December 9th 1975.

HOUSE SPARROW (Passer domesticus) [R], [B]

J F M A M J J A S O N D

Abundant resident found wherever humans are present, except for a few upland farms on the moor. Forms flocks in autumn/winter when seen in fields and hedgerows and along the coast - with up to 150 along the edge of Minehead Golf Course.

TREE SPARROW (Passer montanus) [RB], [RP], [RW]

J F M A M J J A S O N D

Used to breed at Monksilver up to the 1920s, but since then very rare, with only occasional records from the Brendons; otherwise it seems to be absent from Exmoor. The most recent record is of a single bird at Porlock Marsh in the winter of 1989.

CHAFFINCH (Fringilla coelebs) [R], [B], [P], [W]

J F M A M J J A S O N D

Very common, breeding wherever there are trees and bushes, and also common in gardens, parks and farmland. In winter forms large flocks, often with other finches. Winter numbers are swollen largely by influxes of females, from the continent. One record of the central European race F.c. hortensis was identified in the hand, in east Exmoor, November 5th 1959.

BRAMBLING (Fringilla montifringilla) [W], [P]

J F M A M J J A S O N D

Brambling

139

Scarce winter visitor with numbers very variable. Flocks of up to 600 have been seen around Simonsbath, but usually a handful seen in mixed flocks with Chaffinches, from a variety of locations, including gardens. One summer record of a singing male at Culbone Woods, June 22nd-27th 1956.

GREENFINCH (Carduelis chloris) [R], [B], [P]

J F M A M J J A S O N D

Common, breeding in hedges and gardens. Scarce on the high moor, being a summer visitor to some valleys. In autumn and winter forms flocks on stubble and rough fields with numbers up to several hundred, for example 200 in a field at Dunster Beach on October 31st 1989. Passage noticeable most years along the coast west of Minehead.

GOLDFINCH (Carduelis carduelis) [R], [B]

J F M A M J J A S O N D

Fairly common resident although scarce on high ground, and not present in some high valleys in some years. In autumn and winter flocks form up to about 50 but occasionally larger as in 70 plus feeding on seed heads at Dunster Beach, September 19th 1991.

SISKIN (Carduelis spinus) [RR], [RB], [W], [P]

J F M A M J J A S O **N D**

Scarce resident, mainly being a winter visitor and passage migrant. In 1978/1979 a singing male was heard, and breeding was first proved at Luccombe 1979, where it has bred annually since. Has also bred at Dunster (1980) and juveniles have been seen in the breeding season at Alcombe (1989), Mansley Combe (1988), Bagley Combe (1990), and Bratton (1991), and above Luccombe Allers (1992). Flocks of up to 30 regular in winter with an exceptional count of 225 at Dunster Beach, October 30th 1988.

LINNET (Carduelis cannabina) [R], [B]

J F M A M J J A S O N D

Fairly common. Found in North Hill Minehead, Porlock and Valley of Rocks areas, less common on the high moor. In winter birds move to lower ground and flocks form on the coast or inland rough ground, with flocks of up to 50 regular. More unusual were 300-400 on wires at Little Heddon, October 23rd 1987.

TWITE (Carduelis flavirostris) [RW]

J F **M A M J J A S O** N D

Very rare winter visitor, usually recorded singly along the coast, although has been seen inland at Bratton. Small flocks have occurred with 18 at Porlock Marsh, January 5th 1957 and 11 at the same place on February 27th 1975. The most recent record is of two at Dunster Beach, January 27th 1986.

REDPOLL (Carduelis flammea) [B], [R], [W]

J	F	M	A	M	J	J	A	S	O	N	D

Now breeds annually, but breeding numbers fluctuate. Most regular at Croydon Hill, Brendon and the slopes of Dunkery. In winter parties of up to 30 regular and occasionally up to 70 records, also from Hopcott (where there is a regular flock), Webber's Post, Wimbleball, Glenthorne, Timberscombe and Middlecombe.

CROSSBILL (Loxia curvirostra) [RR], [RB]

J	F	M	A	M	J	J	A	S	O	N	D

Irregular visitor to the conifer woods of Exmoor, probably now resident. Has bred, with juveniles at Webber's Post, April 1981 and Wimbleball, June 1980. A singing male was present at Selworthy Hill, May 21st 1988. A handful of records each year of singles or parties of up to 30, from a number of locations including Upper Hopcott, Woodcombe, Periton, Alcombe, Dunster, Culbone, Grabbist and Porlock toll road.

BULLFINCH (Pyrrhula pyrrhula) [R], [B]

| J | F | M | A | M | J | J | A | S | O | N | D |

Fairly common resident, frequently around gardens, hedgerows and orchards. Found on the moorland combes more in autumn when seeds are present.

Bullfinch

143

HAWFINCH (Coccothraustes coccothraustes)
[RR], [RW], [RB]

J F M A M J J A S O N D

Very rare resident and winter visitor. Has nested at Selworthy, but no other breeding records. A few have been seen around the coast in winter. The most recent record is of at least one at Webber's Post, July 3rd 1983.

LAPLAND BUNTING (Calcarius lapponicus) [RW]

J F M **A M J J A** S O N D

Very rare autumn and winter visitor. First record at Porlock Marsh from the end of September 1957 to March 1958. Three at Dunster Beach, January 13th 1980, four at Minehead Golf Course, January 23rd 1987, one at Dunster Beach, November 13th 1989, with one recorded at Wimbleball on March 8th and 12th 1977, and the most recent record from Dunster Beach on March 17th 1990, which was of summer plumage male.

SNOW BUNTING (Plectrophenax nivalis) [W], [P]

J F M A M J J A S O N D

Scarce but regular winter visitor and passage migrant. Most records coastal but occasionally from the moor with two at Dunkery, November 1986, one on November 13th 1992 at the same place, and one at Robin How, October 5th 1988. Most years up to three each for Dunster Beach and Porlock Marsh, between October and March. One September record, on the 5th in 1924.

YELLOWHAMMER (Emberiza citrinella) [R], [B]

J F M A M J J A S O N D

Fairly frequent resident around hedgerows, gorse and bracken-covered hillside and moorland edges, especially in the Brendons, but rare in the high moorland combes. In autumn found in mixed flocks with other finches, and some passage movement noted along the coast.

CIRL BUNTING (Emberiza cirlus) [R], [RB]

J F M A M J J A S O N D

Very rare resident. Has bred in the past around Bossington, in the Porlock Vale, the Minehead district and Combe Martin. Doubtful if it still exists as a breeding species, however, although singing males recorded in the breeding season, most recently at Dunster (April 16th 1987) and Minehead (May 7th 1988). Has been recorded inland as well at Wootton Courtenay and Simonsbath, but not recently. Most regularly recorded along the coast in winter with three in 1989, two at Dunster Beach (November 11th) and one at Bossington (November 1st).

Cirl Bunting

REED BUNTING (Emberiza schoeniclus) [R], [B], [P], [W]

J F M A M J J A S O N D

Fairly common resident, passage migrant and winter visitor. Breeds mainly in marshes, reeds and bogs in places like Wimbleball, Porlock Marsh, Chetsford and Embercombe. In winter small flocks can be found along the coast with other finches especially Linnets. Also regular to some gardens in Minehead and Alcombe in winter.

CORN BUNTING (Miliaria calandra) [V]

| J | F | M | A | M | J | J | A | Ⓢ | O | N | D |

Used to be recorded on the Brendons and around Minehead, but the only record for many years is of a juvenile on Minehead Golf Course, September 9th 1989.

APPENDIX: 'EXOTICS'

Flamingo — one flying west off Dunster Beach, September 12th 1969.

Snow Goose — one regularly seen at Dunster Marsh and Wimbleball with the flock of Canada Geese. Two present from October 11th to 16th 1989.

Emperor Goose — as for Snow Goose but up to five (with three immatures) at Wimbleball, January-December 1987, and three at Dunster Marsh, February 28th 1987. From 1988 onwards only one regularly seen with the Canada Geese at Dunster Beach/Wimbleball.

Bar Headed Goose — one seen regularly with Canada Geese at Minehead/Dunster Marshes 1989-1992.

Ruddy Shelduck — vagrant. Two old records from Porlock Marsh:
- two, November 13th 1915
- one, May 12th 1928.

In recent years no records have been accepted as referring to genuine vagrants. Single birds at Wimbleball, August 10th, August 31st, September 30th and November 12th 1989 (presumably the same bird).

Cape Shelduck — two considered to be this species at Dunster Beach, September 17th - 19th 1987.

Wood Duck — one on Dunster Hawn, March 10th 1987 had been seen for several months previously. One singing male on the River Exe at Brushford, March 17th 1988. A female and four young believed to be this species were seen on the River Barle at Castle Bridge, June 8th 1988.

Sarus Crane — one present around the Brendons area in the mid-1970s was obviously an escapee.

Ring Necked Parakeet — one at Embercombe, August 9th 1985, another at Dunster Beach, October 26th/27th 1989 and one there on November 11th 1990, all likely to have been escapees rather than feral birds.

Black Woodpecker — not accepted on the British List. There were three records around Dunster and Porlock between 1935 and 1944, and a more recent one at Dulverton, May 11th 1987.

EXMOOR SPECIES TOTALS

Species having ever bred	128
Resident breeders	84
Non-resident breeders	30
Non-breeding visitors	93
Species having bred in the past but not regularly any more	15
Species recorded less than ten times	52
Number of species recorded on Exmoor	274

CHECKLIST AND INDEX OF SPECIES RECORDED ON EXMOOR

153

BIBLIOGRAPHY

Hendy E.W., *Somerset Birds and Other Folk.* Eyre & Spottiswoode (1943).

Palmer and Ballance, *The Birds of Somerset.* Longmans (1968).

Allen N.V., *The Birds of Exmoor.* Exmoor Press (1971).

Allen N.V. and Butcher R., *Birds in Exmoor National Park.* E.N.H.S. (1984).

Somerset Ornithological Society, *Birds of Somerset.* Alan Sutton (1988).

Annual Reports of the Somerset Ornithological Society.

The Exmoor Naturalist (Annual Report of the E.N.H.S.).

Annual Reports of the Devon Birdwatching and Preservation Society.

NOTES